180 DAYS™
Phonics
for Kindergarten

Author
Carol Huey-Gatewood, M.A.Ed

Consultant
Lisa Hollis, M.A.Ed.
First Grade Teacher
Sylvan Union School District

Program Credits
Corinne Burton, M.A.Ed., *President* and *Publisher*
Gabe Thibodeau, *Content Director*
Véronique Bos, *VP of Creative*
Lynette Ordoñez, *Content Manager*
Hilary Wolcott, M.A.Ed., *Editor*
Jill Malcolm, *Senior Graphic Designer*

Image Credits: all images from Shutterstock and/or iStock

Standards
© Copyright 2010 National Governors Association Center for Best Practices and Council of Chief State School Officers. All rights reserved.
© Copyright 2007–2024 Texas Education Agency (TEA). All Rights Reserved.
© 2024 TESOL International Association
© 2024 Board of Regents of the University of Wisconsin System

A division of Teacher Created Materials
5482 Argosy Avenue
Huntington Beach, CA 92649-1039
www.tcmpub.com/shell-education
ISBN 978-1-0876-6255-8
© 2025 Shell Educational Publishing, Inc.
Printed by: 51497
Printed in: China

Table of Contents

Introduction

180 Days of Practice

Appendix

What Is Phonics?

Learning to read is a complex process. Students must know the speech sounds associated with written letters in words, how to put those sounds together to form pronounceable words, and how to recognize words rapidly (Beck and Beck 2013). Phonics is a method of instruction that teaches learners the relationship between sounds and letters and how to use those sounds and letters to read and spell. Practice is especially important to help early readers recognize words rapidly. *180 Days™: Phonics* offers teachers and parents a full page of targeted phonics practice activities for each day of the school year.

The Science of Reading

Phonics instruction has historically been at the forefront of much debate and research. The "whole-language" approach presented in the *Dick and Jane* books dominated beginning reading instruction with its "look-say" method that required students to memorize whole words without any attention to decoding (sounding out) words. This method was highly criticized by Rudolf Flesch's 1955 publication *Why Johnny Can't Read* and by Jeanne Chall's 1967 publication *Learning to Read: The Great Debate*. Both researchers indicated the need for direct phonics instruction in place of teaching trial and error and the memorization of whole words. In 1997, Congress commissioned a review of this reading research. The National Reading Panel (NRP) released their report in 2000, which became the backbone of the Science of Reading. The panel's findings clearly showed that, in order for students to become better readers, they need systematic and explicit instruction in these five areas:

- Phonemic Awareness: understanding and manipulating individual speech sounds

- Phonics: matching sounds to letters for use in reading and spelling

- Fluency: reading connected text accurately and smoothly

- Vocabulary: knowing the meanings of words in speech and in print

- Reading Comprehension: understanding what is read

An effective reading program must include instruction in foundational skills, such as phonemic awareness, as well as direct instruction in relating sounds to written letters or sequences of letters that represent those sounds.

Phonics will more than likely continue to play a key role in the Science of Reading. Decades of research have proven it to be the most effective means for building foundational literacy in learners.

What Is Phonics? *(cont.)*

Elements of Instruction

The alphabetic principle is the idea that letters and letter patterns represent the sounds of spoken language. When students who are learning to read and write begin to connect letters (graphemes) with their sounds (phonemes), they have cracked the alphabetic principle. The goal of phonics instruction is to teach students that there are systematic and predictable relationships between written letters and spoken sounds. Learning these predictable relationships allows students to apply the alphabetic principle to both familiar and unfamiliar words and to begin to read with fluency.

Children use their prior learning as a bridge to new learning. For this reason, the best phonics instruction presents skills sequentially from simple to complex. According to Robert Marzano, "Practice has always been, and always will be, a necessary ingredient to learning procedural knowledge at a level at which students execute it independently" (2010, 83). Practice is especially important to help students apply phonics concepts to a wide range of words. Learners need multiple opportunities to review learned skills and to practice the relationship between letters and sound patterns.

Research to Practice

180 Days™: Phonics has been informed by reading research. This series provides opportunities for students to practice the skills that are proven to contribute to reading growth.

- Phonics concepts are presented from **simple to complex** with prior learning embedded within each week. This provides students with **multiple opportunities to practice** target skills.

- Daily practices intentionally build upon one another to help students **bridge new learning** to prior concepts.

- Specific **language comprehension** and **word-recognition skills** are reinforced throughout the activities.

- An overview page is provided before each unit to introduce key concepts and provide **explicit instructional strategies**.

- **Phonemic awareness** and **phonological awareness** are embedded within the progression of skills and concepts.

- Students read and write words with target concepts to reinforce the connection between **graphemes** and **phonemes**.

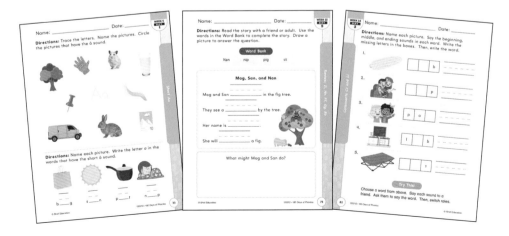

How to Use This Resource

Unit Structure Overview

This resource is divided into 9 units. Each unit focuses on a specific phonics concept. This provides ample practice with each concept before moving on to more complex patterns.

Unit	Week	Focus
Unit 1: Concepts of Print	1–4	Concept of a Letter, Concept of a Word, First and Last Letter, Letter vs. Word, Word vs. Sentence, Letter-Sound Connection
Unit 2: Short *Aa*	5	Short *Aa*
	6	Consonants: *Mm, Tt*
	7	Consonants: *Ss, Pp*
	8	Review: *Aa, Mm, Tt, Ss, Pp*
Unit 3: Short *Ii*	9	Short *Ii*
	10	Consonants: *Nn, Ff*
	11	Consonants: *Gg, Bb*
	12	Review: *Ii, Nn, Ff, Gg, Bb*
Unit 4: Short *Oo*	13	Short *Oo*
	14	Consonants: *Cc, Ll*
	15	Consonants: *Hh, Jj*
	16	Review: *Oo, Cc, Ll, Hh, Jj*
Unit 5: Short *Uu*	17	Short *Uu*
	18	Consonants: *Rr, Kk* (spelling *ck*)
	19	Consonants: *Dd, Yy*
	20	Review: *Uu, Rr, Kk, Dd, Yy*

Unit	Week	Focus
Unit 6: Short *Ee*	21	Short *Ee*
	22	Consonants: *Qq, Ww*
	23	Consonants: *Vv, Xx, Zz*
	24	Review: *Ee, Qq, Vv, Ww, Xx, Zz*
Unit 7: CVC Words	25	Short *Aa* Words (*ab, at, am, an, ap*)
	26	Short *Ii* Words (*ig, id, im, in, it, ip*)
	27	Short *Oo* Words (*og, op, ob, ot*)
	28	Short *Uu* Words (*ug, ub, ut, un, um*)
	29	Short *Ee* Words (*et, en, eg, eb, ed*)
	30	Review: CVC Words
Unit 8: Long Vowels	31	Long *Aa* and Long *Ii*
	32	Long *Ee* and Long *Oo*
	33	Long *Uu* (normal and glided)
	34	Review: Long Vowels
Unit 9: Cumulative Review	35	Review: Consonants and Short Vowels
	36	Review: CVC Words

How to Use This Resource *(cont.)*

Overview Pages

Each unit follows a consistent format for ease of use. An overview page introduces phonics concepts at the beginning of each unit. These pages support family understanding and provide opportunities to prepare students for the activities presented in the following practice pages. Teachers may wish to send the page home with students at the beginning of each unit to inform parents of what is being learned at school.

A box at the top of each page explains the phonics concept presented in the unit.

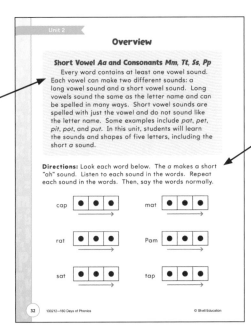

An introductory activity provides an example of a strategy used within the unit or addresses common misconceptions with a specific phonics skill. Complete this activity as a class or in small groups to help prepare students for the upcoming topics.

How to Use This Resource (cont.)

Student Practice Pages

Practice pages reinforce grade-level phonics skills. This book provides one practice page for each day of the school year. Each day's phonics activity is provided as a full practice page, making it easy to prepare and implement as part of a morning routine, at the beginning of each phonics lesson, or as homework.

Day 1 of each week teaches students the phonics focus of the week and how to identify the target sound.

On **Day 2**, students isolate beginning, middle, or end phonemes.

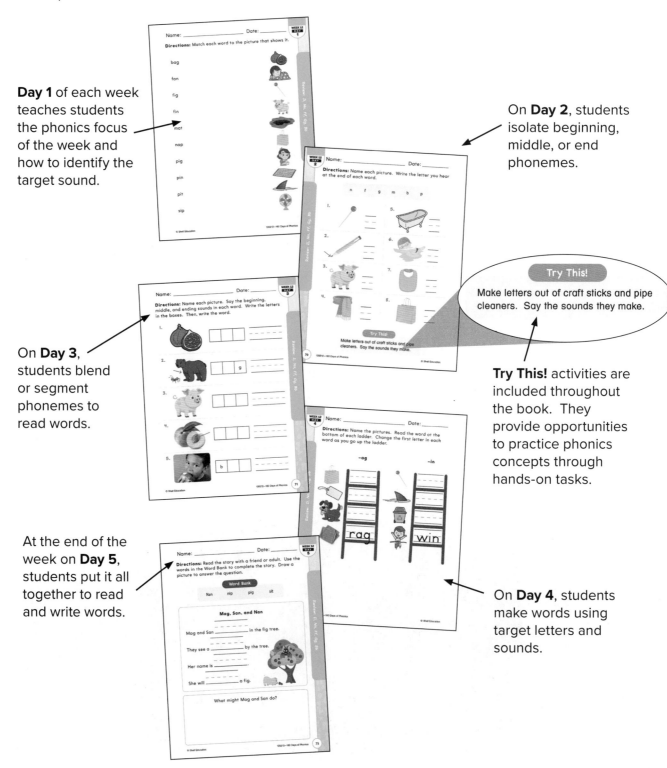

Try This!

Make letters out of craft sticks and pipe cleaners. Say the sounds they make.

On **Day 3**, students blend or segment phonemes to read words.

Try This! activities are included throughout the book. They provide opportunities to practice phonics concepts through hands-on tasks.

At the end of the week on **Day 5**, students put it all together to read and write words.

On **Day 4**, students make words using target letters and sounds.

How to Use This Resource *(cont.)*

Digital Resources

Several resources are provided digitally. (See page 216 for instructions on how to download these pages.) These tools provide additional phonics support. These tools include the following:

- **Standards Correlations**—This resource shows how the activities align with key standards.

- **Class and Individual Analysis Sheets**—These analysis sheets can be used to track student progress toward mastery of concepts. Results can be analyzed to determine next steps for differentiating instruction to meet varying student needs.

- **Hands-On Letter Practice**—These large uppercase and lowercase letters include formation arrows. This makes it the perfect tool for students to practice with their fingers or with pencils.

- **Writing Practice**—These pages include dotted uppercase and lowercase letters on writing lines.

Instructional Options

180 Days™: Phonics is a flexible resource that can be used in various instructional settings for different purposes.

- Use the practice pages as daily warm-up activities.

- Work with students in small groups, allowing them to focus on specific skills. This setting also lends itself to partner and group discussions about the phonics focus.

- Practice pages in this resource can be completed independently during center times and as activities for early finishers.

How to Use This Resource (cont.)

Diagnostic Assessment

The practice pages in this book can be used as diagnostic assessments. These activity pages require students to identify specific phonics concepts within words, read connected text, and write responses using target concepts. (An answer key for the practice pages is provided starting on page 203.)

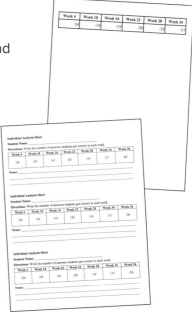

Analysis sheets are provided as Microsoft Word® and Microsoft Excel® files in the digital resources. There is a Class Analysis Sheet and an Individual Analysis Sheet. Use the file that matches your assessment needs. At the end of a unit, count the number of problems students got correct for the last week and enter it into the chart. Analyze the data on the analysis sheet to determine instructional focuses for your child or class.

The diagnostic analysis tools included in the digital resources allow for quick evaluation and ongoing monitoring of student work. See at a glance which phonics concepts students may need to explore further to develop fluency.

Using the Results to Differentiate Instruction

Once results are gathered and analyzed, use the data to determine how to differentiate instruction. The data can help determine which concepts are the most difficult for students, as well as identify students who need additional instructional support and continued practice.

The results of the diagnostic analysis may show that an entire class is struggling with a particular phonics concept. If these concepts have been taught in the past, this indicates that further instruction or reteaching is necessary. If these concepts have not been taught yet, this data is a great preassessment and demonstrates that students do not have a working knowledge of the concepts.

The results of the diagnostic analysis may also show that an individual or small group of students is struggling with a particular concept or group of concepts. Consider pulling aside these students to instruct further on the concept(s) while others work independently. You can also use the results to help identify individuals or groups of proficient students who are ready for enrichment or above-grade-level instruction. These students may benefit from independent learning contracts or more challenging activities.

Overview

Concepts of Print and Phonemic Awareness

Concepts of print are foundational skills for literacy. They include the awareness that print has meaning and directionality and that words are made of individual letters. In this unit, students will learn about the following concepts of print:

- each letter has a shape and a name
- a word is a group of letters that has meaning
- words contain first and last letters
- sentences are groups of words that make sense
- there are spaces between words in a sentence
- sentences end with punctuation
- letters make sounds

Directions: Look at the alphabet. Listen to and say the name of each letter. There is a capital and lowercase letter for each one. The red letters are vowels. Every word has at least one vowel.

Aa	Bb	Cc	Dd	Ee	Ff	Gg
Hh	Ii	Jj	Kk	Ll	Mm	Nn
Oo	Pp	Qq	Rr	Ss	Tt	Uu
Vv	Ww	Xx	Yy	Zz		

Name: _____ Date: _____

Directions: Touch each letter. Sing the ABC song. Say the names of the pictures on the chart. Then, circle the first letter of each word.

Aa	Bb	Cc	Dd	Ee	Ff	Gg
apple	bat	car	dog	elephant	feather	grapes

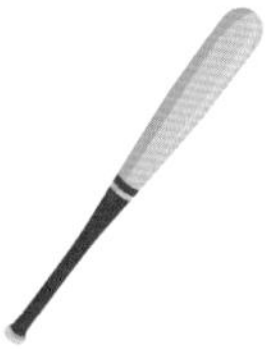

Hh	Ii	Jj	Kk	Ll	Mm	Nn
horse	iguana	jellyfish	kangaroo	lion	mouse	nut

Oo	Pp	Qq	Rr	Ss	Tt	Uu
octopus	pig	queen	rainbow	snake	tiger	umbrella

Vv	Ww	Xx	Yy	Zz
violin	whale	x-ray	yo-yo	zebra

Try This!

Name letters or words from the chart. Have a friend point to the matching boxes. Then, switch places!

Directions: Look at the letter pairs. Touch the places that show how the letters are different. Then, say the names of the letters.

a o   i l

f t   m n

d b   q p

Directions: Name each fruit. Circle the first letter in each word. Name the letters. Then, color the pictures.

apple   grapes   banana

Name: _____ Date: _____

Directions: Say the letter names. Find the letters in the picture. Then, color the picture using the key.

Color Code

w	v	p	g	j
brown	red	blue	yellow	green

Directions: Listen to the sentence. Circle the first and last letters in Pam's name. Then, say the names of the letters.

Pam can read on a mat.

Concept of a Letter

Directions: Name each letter. Draw lines to match the letters.

A   s

M   b

T   t

S   a

P   g

I   n

N   i

F   f

G   p

B   m

Concept of a Letter

Directions: Write your name. Make the first letter a capital. Say the names of the letters. Then, circle the first and last letters.

_____

_ _ _ _ _ _ _ _ _ _ _ _ _ _ _ _ _ _ _ _

_____

Name: _____   Date: _____

Directions: Say the names of the pictures. Circle the first letters in the words. Write the first letters on the lines. Then, color the pictures.

1.

_____

_ _

cat   ____at

2.

_____

_ _

lion   ____ion

3.

_____

_ _

hippo   ____ippo

4.

_____

_ _

rabbit   ____abbit

5.

_____

_ _

dog   ____og

6.

_____

_ _

turtle   ____urtle

Try This!

Draw an animal. Write the name of the animal. Then, circle the first letter in the word.

Name: _____ Date: _____

Directions: Name each color. Circle the first letter in each color word. Then, underline each word.

yellow

orange

purple

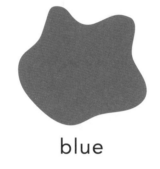

blue

red

black

green

Concept of a Word

Directions: Your name is a word! Names begin with capital letters. Write your first name. Circle the first and last letters in your name. Say the letters in your name. Count the letters in your name.

_____

_ _ _ _ _ _ _ _ _ _ _ _ _ _ _ _ _ _ _ _

_____

Name: _____ Date: _____

Directions: Color the words blue. Circle the letters that are not part of words. Name those letters.

Concept of a Word

a   i   jog

in   h

at

x   pen

hum   r

k

z   Sam

Try This!

Write the two letters that can also be words. Make them capitals.

___ ___

___ ___

___ ___

Directions: Write the first letter of each word.

1.

___ ___
_ _

map   ___ap

3.

___ ___
_ _

fan   ___an

2.

___ ___
_ _

Sam   ___am

4.

___ ___
_ _

pig   ___ig

Directions: Write the last letter of each word.

5.

___ ___
_ _

man   ma___

7.

___ ___
_ _

tap   ta___

6.

___ ___
_ _

Pam   Pa___

8.

___ ___
_ _

big   bi___

Concept of a Word

Name: _____   Date: _____

Directions: Circle the first and last letter in each word. Then, write the letters in the chart.

Concept of a Word

1.

nap

2.

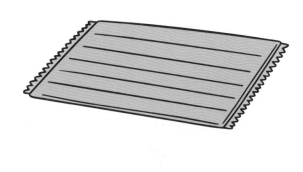

mat

3.

jam

4.

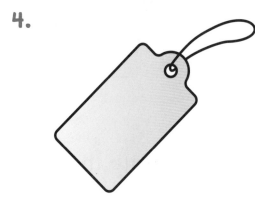

tag

First Letters	Last Letters

Name: _____ Date: _____

Directions: Say the name of each picture. Say the first letter of each picture. Circle the word that matches.

Picture	First Letter	Word		
1.	d	car	doll	lad
2.	p	sap	goat	pencil
3.	h	hat	bear	park
4.	c	sack	cow	bog

Directions: Put an *X* between each word in the sentences. Count the words.

5. I   can   learn.

6. The   dog   jumps.

7. The   cat   naps.

Name: _____ Date: _____

Directions: Name the pictures. Use the Word Bank to write the missing letters. Then, color the pictures.

Words and Sentences

Word Bank

bed   cab   fig   fin   ham   rat

1.

_____

_ _

_____ig

2.

_____

_ _

_____ab

3.

_____

_ _

ha_____

4.

_____

_ _

be_____

5.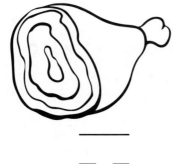

_____

_ _

ra_____

6.

_____

_ _

fi_____

Name: _____ Date: _____

Directions: Say the first and last letters in the words. Then, draw lines to match the words.

sock   **Hen**

tin   **bud**

Jam   **Sock**

Bud   **Tin**

hen   **jam**

Directions: Underline the words in each sentence. Circle the capital letter at the beginning of each sentence. Circle the period at the end.

1.

Pat likes jam.

3.

The hen eats.

2.

He puts on a sock.

4.

His name is Bud.

Name: _____   Date: _____

Directions: Circle the words in the picture. Circle the same words in the sentences. Read the sentences with a friend or adult. Then, color the picture.

Words and Sentences

The jar has a lid.   I can run.

I met a girl.   The cat is big.

Tom likes the dog.   Did your hair get wet?

Try This!

Look at sentences in your favorite book. Point to the spaces between the words. Point to the capital letters. Look for the periods, question marks, and exclamation points. Talk to an adult about what each one means.

Name: _____ Date: _____

Directions: Read each sentence with a friend or adult. Write a word from the Word Bank to finish each sentence. Circle the first and last words in each sentence.

Word Bank

cat   map   pup   red   run

1. I made a _____ .

2. The van is _____ .

3. A _____ can sit.

4. Can he _____ ?

5. The _____ is on a lap.

Words and Sentences

Name: _____ Date: _____

Directions: Read the sentence with an adult. Read it again. Clap your hands for each word. Count the words, and write the number. Circle the exclamation point. Then, read the sentence again using an excited voice.

We all scream for ice cream!

_____
_ _ _

How many words? _____

....

Directions: Draw an ice cream that you would like to eat.

Name: _____ Date: _____

Directions: Say the names of the pictures. Say the first sound you hear in each name. Then, circle the vowels *Aa*, *Ee*, *Ii*, *Oo*, and *Uu*.

Aa	Bb	Cc	Dd	Ee	Ff	Gg
apple	bat	car	dog	elephant	feather	grapes
Hh	Ii	Jj	Kk	Ll	Mm	Nn
horse	iguana	jellyfish	kangaroo	lion	mouse	nut
Oo	Pp	Qq	Rr	Ss	Tt	Uu
octopus	pig	queen	rainbow	snake	tiger	umbrella
Vv	Ww	Xx	Yy	Zz		
violin	whale	x-ray	yo-yo	zebra		

Letter-Sound Connections

Name: _____ Date: _____

Directions: Name the pictures. Draw a line to the letter you hear at the beginning of each word. Then, color the pictures.

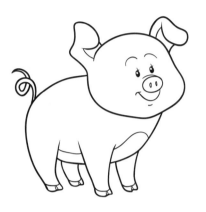

M

T

S

N

P

Name: _____ Date: _____

Directions: Name the pictures. Draw a line to the letter you hear at the beginning of each word. Then, color the pictures.

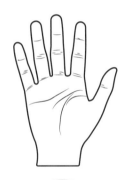

g

b

c

l

h

f

Name: _____ Date: _____

Directions: Say each letter. Say the sound it makes. Then, follow the steps to color the pictures.

Jj   Rr   Kk   Dd   Yy

Color the picture that starts with *j* orange.

Color the picture that starts with *r* blue.

Color the picture that starts with *k* red.

Color the picture that starts with *d* brown.

Color the picture that starts with *y* purple.

Letter-Sound Connections

Directions: Say each letter. Say the sound it makes. Then, follow the steps to color the pictures.

Qq   Ww   Vv   Xx   Zz

Color the picture that starts with *q* yellow.

Color the picture that starts with *w* **purple**.

Color the picture that starts with *v* orange.

Color the picture that starts with *x* pink.

Color the picture that starts with *z* green.

Letter–Sound Connections

Overview

Short Vowel *Aa* and Consonants *Mm*, *Tt*, *Ss*, and *Pp*

Every word contains at least one vowel sound. Each vowel can make two different sounds: a long vowel sound and a short vowel sound. Long vowels sound the same as the letter name and can be spelled in many ways. Short vowel sounds are spelled with just the vowel and do not sound like the letter name. Some examples include *pat*, *vet*, *pit*, *not*, and *tub*.

In this unit, students will learn the sounds and shapes of five letters, including the short *a* sound.

Directions: Look at each word. The *a* makes a short "ah" sound. Listen to each sound in the words. Repeat each sound in the words. Then, say the words normally.

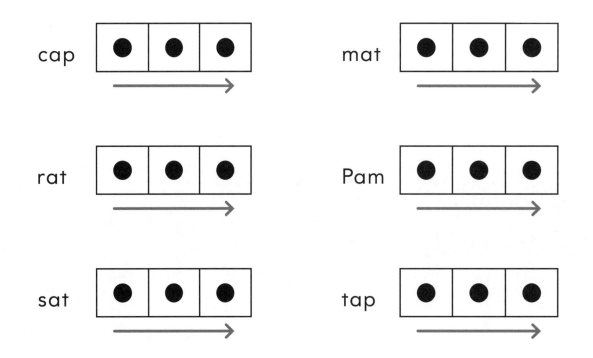

cap

mat

rat

Pam

sat

tap

Name: _____ Date: _____

Directions: Trace the letters. Name the pictures. Circle the pictures that have the ă sound.

Directions: Name each picture. Write the letter *a* in the words that have the short ă sound.

b____g   s____n   p____t   n____p

Name: _____ Date: _____

Directions: Color the letters. Name the pictures. Say the sound you hear at the beginning of each word. Circle the pictures that start with the ă sound.

. . . .

Directions: Draw something that begins with the ă sound. Label your picture.

Name: _____ Date: _____

Directions: Say the name of each picture. Listen for the ă sound in each word. Write an *a* in one box to show if it is the beginning, middle, or ending sound. Then, color the pictures.

1.

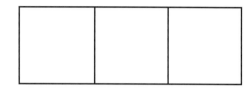

2.

3.

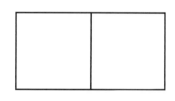

4.
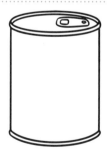
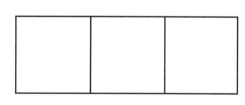

5.
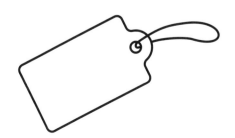

Short Aa

Name: _____ Date: _____

Directions: Trace the letters. Name the pictures. Listen for the ă sound in the words. Color the flowers that have pictures with the ă sound. Follow the flower path to find the kitten!

Short Aa

130212—180 Days™: Phonics   © Shell Education

Name: _____ Date: _____

Directions: Write the letter *a* on each line. Read the sentences with a friend or adult. Circle the words with the ă sound. Draw a picture for each sentence.

1.

_____
_ _
The h_____t is on the bed.

2.

_____ _____
_ _ _ _
The c_____t s_____t.

3.

_____ _____
_ _ _ _
The b_____t c_____n fly.

4.

_____ _____
_ _ _ _
The m_____t is bl_____ck.

Short Aa

Try This!

How many words can you rhyme with *cat*? How many words can you rhyme with *fan*? What other words can you rhyme?

Name: _____   Date: _____

Directions: Trace the letters. Name the pictures. Draw a line to the letter you hear at the beginning of each word.

Directions: Draw something that starts with *m*. Then, draw something that starts with *t*.

Name: _____ Date: _____

Directions: Name each picture. Write the letter you hear at the beginning of each word.

1.  __ __ __

5. 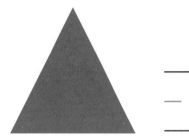 __ __ __

2. 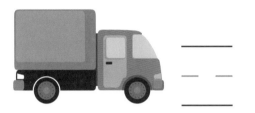 __ __ __

6.  __ __ __

3. 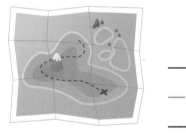 __ __ __

7. 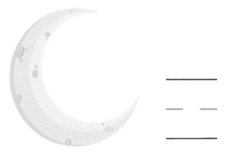 __ __ __

4.  __ __ __

8.  __ __ __

Try This!

Cover a flat surface with shaving cream, sand, or clay. Form the letters *M* and *m* while saying /m/. Form the letters *T* and *t* while saying /t/.

Name: _____ Date: _____

Directions: Touch each dot, and say the sound. Read the word. Write the word. Then, color the pictures.

1.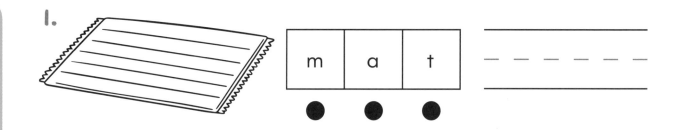

2.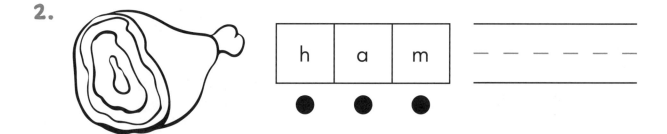

3.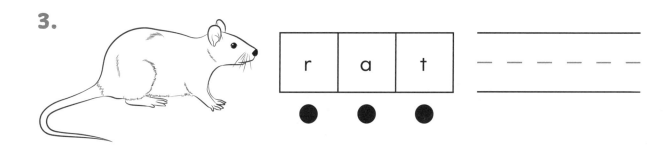

4.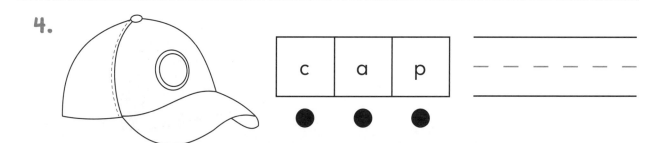

Try This!

Form small balls with clay. Place the balls into the boxes. Squish each ball as you say the sound. Run your finger under the boxes as you read the word.

Directions: Write the letter *a* on the line. Say each sound. Read the word. Write the word on the line.

1.

t ___ p _____

3.

m ___ t _____

2.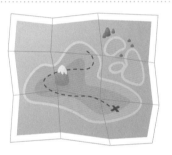

m ___ p _____

4.

T ___ m _____

Directions: Read the sentence. Then, answer the question.

Tam sat on the mat.

_____

5. What did Tam sit on? _____

Consonants *Mm* and *Tt*

Name: _____   Date: _____

Directions: Read the story with a friend or adult. Underline words with the ă sound. Circle the picture that answers the question.

I am Tam.

My map is on a mat.

The mat is by the tub.

The map is wet.

I am mad.

Why is Tam mad?

The mat is by the tub.

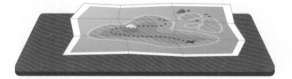

The map is on the mat.

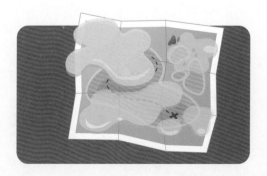

The map is wet.

Name: _____ Date: _____

Directions: Trace the letters. Say the words. Write each word in the chart. Then, color the pictures.

Pam

sap

sat

Sam

pat

Ss

Pp

Starts with **S**	Starts with **P**

Name: _____ Date: _____

Directions: Color the letters. Name the pictures. Write the letter you hear at the beginning of each word.

··

Directions: Name each picture. Write the letter you hear at the end of each word.

Name: _____ Date: _____

Directions: Touch each dot, and say the sound. Read the word. Write the word. Then, color the pictures.

1.

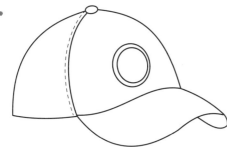

c	a	p

● ● ●

_____

2.

S	a	l

● ● ●

_____

3.

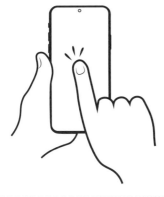

t	a	p

● ● ●

_____

4.

p	a	l

● ● ●

_____

Consonants *Ss* and *Pp*

Name: _____ Date: _____

Directions: Name the pictures. Read the words on the ladders. Draw lines from the pictures to the matching words.

-at

mat

pat

sat

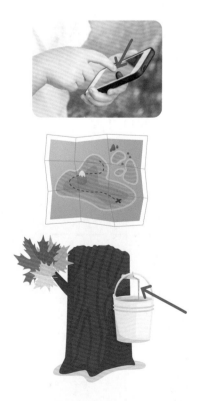

-ap

map

sap

tap

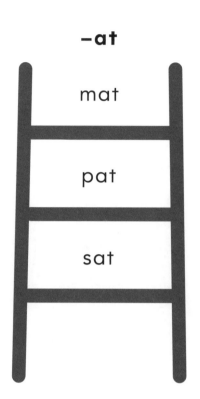

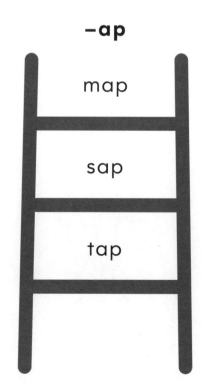

Directions: Read the story with a friend or adult. Use the words in the Word Bank to complete the story. Draw a picture to go with the story.

Word Bank

cat   nap   sat   Pat   mat

Pat has a _____.

The cat has a red _____.

The cat takes a _____ on the mat.

Did _____ nap with the cat?

No, he _____!

Consonants Ss and Pp

Name: _____ Date: _____

Directions: Read the words in the picture. Look at the first letter of each word. Find those letters in the key. Color the picture using the key.

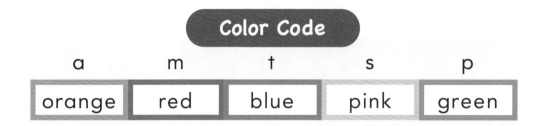

Color Code

a	m	t	s	p
orange	red	blue	pink	green

130212—180 Days™: Phonics   © Shell Education

Name: _____ Date: _____

Directions: Name each picture. Listen to the first sound in each word. Circle the picture that does not belong in each row.

1.

2.

3.

4.

5.

Review: Aa, Mm, Tt, Ss, Pp

WEEK 8 DAY 3

Name: _____ Date: _____

Directions: Name each picture. Say the beginning, middle, and ending sounds in each word. Write the letters in the boxes. Then, write the word.

Review: Aa, Mm, Tt, Ss, Pp

1.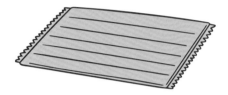

2.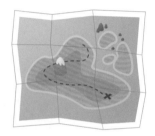
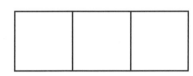

3.

| t | | |

4.

| | a | |

5.

| | | p |

© Shell Education

Name: _____   Date: _____

Directions: Name the pictures. Write the missing letters.
Then, read the words.

–ap

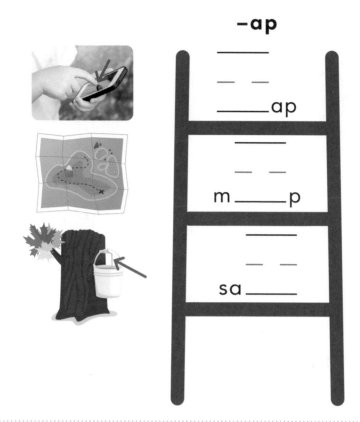

_____
_ _
_____ap

_____
_ _
m _____ p

_____
_ _
sa _____

–at

_____
_ _
p _____ t

_____
_ _
sa _____

_____
_ _
_____at

Name: _____ Date: _____

Directions: Read each sentence. Look at each picture. Circle whether the picture matches each sentence.

1.

Sam sat on his hat.

yes　　　no

3.

The sap is black.

yes　　　no

2.

Pat is at the van.

yes　　　no

4.

Pam can pat the cat.

yes　　　no

Directions: Finish the sentence. Draw a picture to go with it.

_____

_ _ _ _ _ _

I can _____.

Overview

Short Vowel *Ii* and Consonants *Nn*, *Ff*, *Gg*, and *Bb*

Word families are groups of words that have similar combinations of letters and sounds. For example, *at*, *cat*, *hat*, and *mat* are a family of words with the "at" combination. Learning word families helps readers understand and analyze word patterns. Knowing these patterns will help beginning readers recognize similar words.

Directions: Look at the words. The *i* makes a short "ih" sound. Listen to each sound in the words. Repeat each sound in the words. Then, say the words normally.

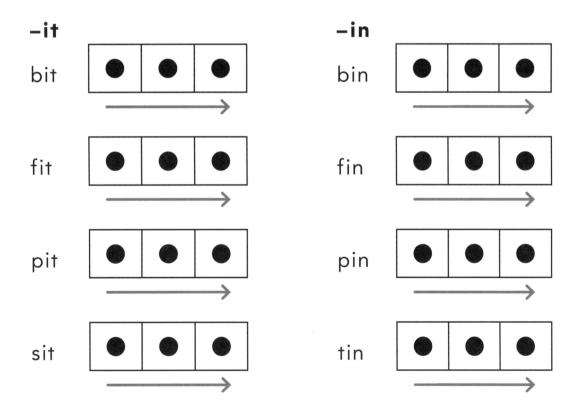

–it

bit

fit

pit

sit

–in

bin

fin

pin

tin

Name: _____   Date: _____

Directions: Color the letters. Name the pictures. Write *i* on the lines to complete the words.

1.

_____

__   __

n_____p

2.

_____

__   __

s_____p

3.

_____

__   __

b_____t

4.

_____

__   __

s_____t

5.

_____

__   __

p_____t

6.

_____

__   __

T_____m

Name: _____ Date: _____

Directions: Trace the letters. Name the pictures. Listen for the ĭ sound in the words. Color the rocks that have pictures with the ĭ sound. Follow the path to find the treasure!

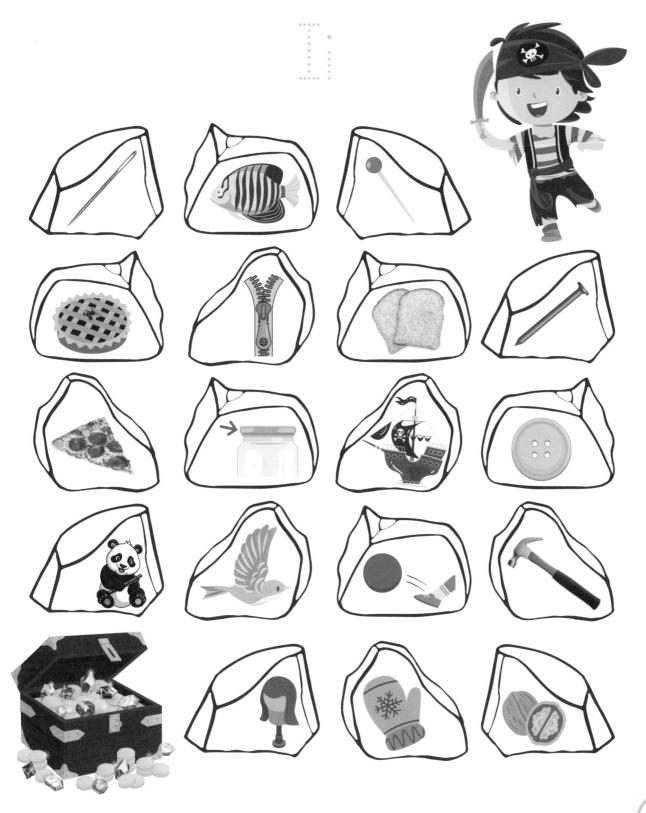

Short Ii

Name: _____ Date: _____

Directions: Touch each dot, and say the sound. Read the word. Write the word. Then, color the pictures.

1.
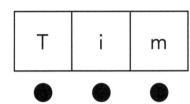

T	i	m
● ● ●

2.
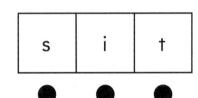

s	i	t
● ● ●

3.
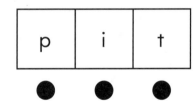

p	i	t
● ● ●

4.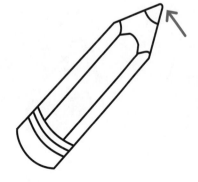

t	i	p
● ● ●

Directions: Name the pictures. Write the missing letters.
Then, read the words.

–it

___ ___ ___

b ___ ___ ___

___ ___ ___

___ ___ t

___ ___ ___

___ i ___

–ip

___ ___ ___

r ___ ___ ___

___ ___ ___

___ i ___

___ ___ ___

t ___ ___ ___

Short *Ii*

. . . .

Directions: Read the sentence. Write a word from the
word ladders. Draw a picture.

___ ___ ___

___ ___ ___ ___

Tim jumps over the p ___ ___ ___ .

Name: _____   Date: _____

Short Ii

Directions: Read the story with a friend or adult. Circle the words with short *a* and short *i* sounds. Write the words in the chart. Draw a picture to go with the story. Then, read the story aloud.

Pat and Tim

Pat can sit by the water.

She can sit by Tim on the mat.

Pat and Tim look at the map.

They see a pit on the map.

Short *a*	Short *i*

Name: _____ Date: _____

Directions: Trace the letters. Name each picture. Then, write the letter you hear at the beginning of each word.

Nn   Ff

1.    ____ ____ ____

2.    ____ ____ ____

3.    ____ ____ ____

4.    ____ ____ ____

5.    ____ ____ ____

6.   ____ ____ ____

7.    ____ ____ ____

8.    ____ ____ ____

Consonants *Nn* and *Ff*

Directions: Draw something that starts with *n*. Then, draw something that starts with *f*.

Name: _____ Date: _____

Directions: Color the letters. Name the pictures. Then, write the letter you hear at the end of each word.

Nn Ff

1.  ___ ___

5. 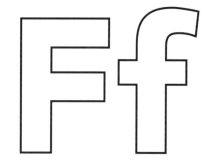 ___ ___

2.  ___ ___

6.  ___ ___

3.  ___ ___

7.  ___ ___

4. 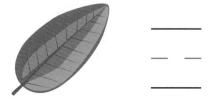 ___ ___

8.  ___ ___

Try This!

How many words can you rhyme with *fin*? How many words can you rhyme with *pit*? What other words can you rhyme?

Name: _____ Date: _____

Directions: Name each picture. Say the beginning, middle, and ending sounds in each word. Write the letters in the boxes. Then, write the word.

1.

2.

3.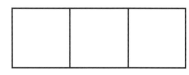

4.

5.

Consonants Nn and Ff

Name: _____   Date: _____

Directions: Name each picture. Connect three letters to make the word. Write the word.

1.    m   f   _____
       a   ‑ ‑ ‑ ‑ ‑ ‑ ‑ ‑
    n   p   _____

2.    f   s   _____
       a   ‑ ‑ ‑ ‑ ‑ ‑ ‑ ‑
    t   n   _____

3.    t   p   _____
       i   ‑ ‑ ‑ ‑ ‑ ‑ ‑ ‑
    n   s   _____

4.    m   s   _____
       a   ‑ ‑ ‑ ‑ ‑ ‑ ‑ ‑
    f   n   _____

5.    n   i   _____
       a   ‑ ‑ ‑ ‑ ‑ ‑ ‑ ‑
    m   t   _____

6.    t   n   _____
       a   ‑ ‑ ‑ ‑ ‑ ‑ ‑ ‑
    p   i   _____

Directions: Write a sentence about Nin and Fin.

   _____

       ‑ ‑ ‑ ‑ ‑ ‑ ‑ ‑ ‑ ‑ ‑ ‑ ‑ ‑ ‑ ‑ ‑ ‑

    _____

Directions: Name the pictures. Read the words. Use the words to write sentences about the pictures. Read the sentences aloud. Then, color the pictures.

1.    The   can

   sit.   bat

_____
— — — — — — — — — — — —
_____
_____
— — — — — — — — — — — —
_____

2. 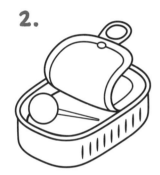   pin   a

   in   is

   The   tin.

_____
— — — — — — — — — — — —
_____
_____
— — — — — — — — — — — —
_____

3.    has   San

   fan.

   a   tan

_____
— — — — — — — — — — — —
_____
_____
— — — — — — — — — — — —
_____

4.    Tan   pit.

   the   has

_____
— — — — — — — — — — — —
_____
_____
— — — — — — — — — — — —
_____

Name: _____ Date: _____

Directions: Name the pictures. Circle the pictures that start with the letters on the left.

g				
b				
n				
f				
p				

130212—180 Days™: Phonics

Directions: Name each picture. Circle the letter you hear at the beginning of each word.

1.

g   b

5.

g   b

2.

g   b

6.

g   b

3.

g   b

7.

g   b

4.

g   b

8.

g   b

Directions: Name each picture. Write the letter you hear at the end of each word.

9.

_____

10.

_____

Consonants Gg and Bb

Name: _____ Date: _____

Directions: Touch each dot, and say the sound. Read the word. Write the word. Then, color the pictures.

1.  | b | i | g | ● ● ● _____

2.  | b | a | g | ● ● ● _____

3.  | b | i | n | ● ● ● _____

4.  | g | a | b | ● ● ● _____

5.   | f | i | g | ● ● ● _____

Try This!

What words can you rhyme with *big*? What words can you rhyme with *tin*? What other words can you rhyme?

Name: _____ Date: _____

Directions: Name each picture. Say the beginning, middle, and ending sounds you hear in the word. Use the letters to write the word. Then, color the pictures.

1.

pga

_____

- - - - - - - - - - -

_____

4.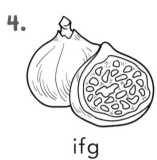

ifg

_____

- - - - - - - - - - -

_____

7.

abg

_____

- - - - - - - - - - -

_____

2.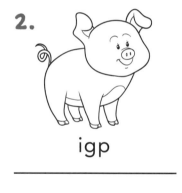

igp

_____

- - - - - - - - - - -

_____

5.

tga

_____

- - - - - - - - - - -

_____

8.

gib

_____

- - - - - - - - - - -

_____

3.

gba

_____

- - - - - - - - - - -

_____

6.

nbi

_____

- - - - - - - - - - -

_____

9.

atb

_____

- - - - - - - - - - -

_____

Consonants *Gg* and *Bb*

Name: _____ Date: _____

Directions: Read the story with a friend or adult. Use the words in the Word Bank to complete the story. Draw a picture to answer the question.

Word Bank

bat   figs   San   sit

Mag and San

_____

— — — — — — —

Mag is a black _____.

_____

— — — — — — —

She likes to gab with _____.

_____

— — — — — — —

She likes to _____ with San.

_____

— — — — — — —

She and San like _____.

What do Mag and San like to do?

Name: _____ Date: _____

Directions: Match each word to the picture that shows it.

bag

fan

fig

fin

mat

nap

pig

pin

pit

sip

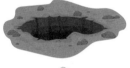

Name: _____ Date: _____

Directions: Name each picture. Write the letter you hear at the end of each word.

n   f   g   m   b   p

1.
_____
_ _
_____

5.

_____
_ _
_____

2.
_____
_ _
_____

6.

_____
_ _
_____

3.

_____
_ _
_____

7.
_____
_ _
_____

4.
_____
_ _
_____

8.

_____
_ _
_____

Try This!

Make letters out of craft sticks and pipe cleaners. Say the sounds they make.

Name: _____ Date: _____

Directions: Name each picture. Say the beginning, middle, and ending sounds in each word. Write the letters in the boxes. Then, write the word.

1.

- - - - - - - -

2.

		g

- - - - - - - -

3.

- - - - - - - -

4.

- - - - - - - -

5.

b		

- - - - - - - -

Name: _____ Date: _____

Directions: Name the pictures. Read the word at the bottom of each ladder. Change the first letter in each word as you go up the ladder.

–ag

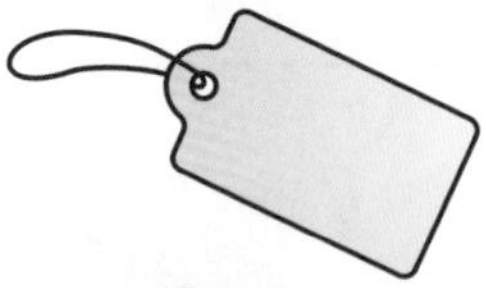

–in

Review: Ii, Nn, Ff, Gg, Bb

rag

win

Name: _____ Date: _____

Directions: Read the story with a friend or adult. Use the words in the Word Bank to complete the story. Draw a picture to answer the question.

Word Bank

Nan   nip   pig   sit

Mag, San, and Nan

_____

Mag and San _____ in the fig tree.

_____

They see a _____ by the tree.

_____

Her name is _____.

_____

She will _____ a fig.

What might Mag and San do?

© Shell Education   130212—180 Days™: Phonics   73

Overview

Short Vowel *Oo* and Consonants *Cc*, *Ll*, *Hh*, and *Jj*

Word families are made up of words that rhyme. To recognize rhymes, students must listen for the similarities. Rhyming words have matching ending sounds that start with the final vowel in the words (*pot*, *hot*). The word families in this unit contain one-syllable words that rhyme.

Directions: Look at the words. The *o* makes a short "aw" sound. Listen to each sound in the words. Repeat each sound in the words. Then, say the words normally.

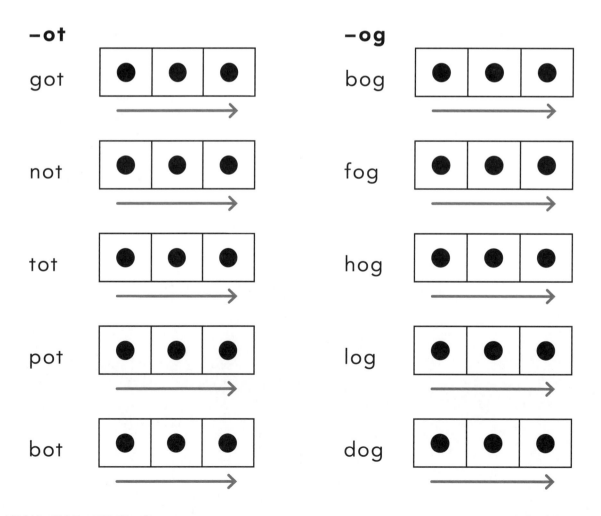

–ot
got
not
tot
pot
bot

–og
bog
fog
hog
log
dog

Directions: Trace the letters. Name the pictures. Circle the pictures that have the ŏ sound.

· ·

Directions: Read the sentence. Underline the words that have the ŏ sound. Draw a picture to go with the sentence.

The log has a pot on top.

Name: _____ Date: _____

Directions: Name the pictures. Listen to the middle sound of each word. Circle the picture that has a different middle sound in each row.

1.

2.

3.

4.

5.

Directions: Name each picture. Write the letter for the middle sound you hear in each word.

6.  ___ ___ ___

9.  ___ ___ ___

7.  ___ ___ ___

10.  ___ ___ ___

8.  ___ ___ ___

11.  ___ ___ ___

Name: _____ Date: _____

Directions: Touch each dot, and say the sound. Read the word. Then, draw a line from each word to the matching picture.

1.

m	o	p

● ● ●

2.

o	n

● ●

3.

f	o	g

● ● ●

4.

m	o	m

● ● ●

5.

t	o	p

● ● ●

6.

s	o	b

● ● ●

Short *Oo*

Name: _____ Date: _____

Directions: Name the pictures. Read the word at the bottom of each ladder. Change the first letter in each word as you go up the ladder.

Short *Oo*

−op   −og

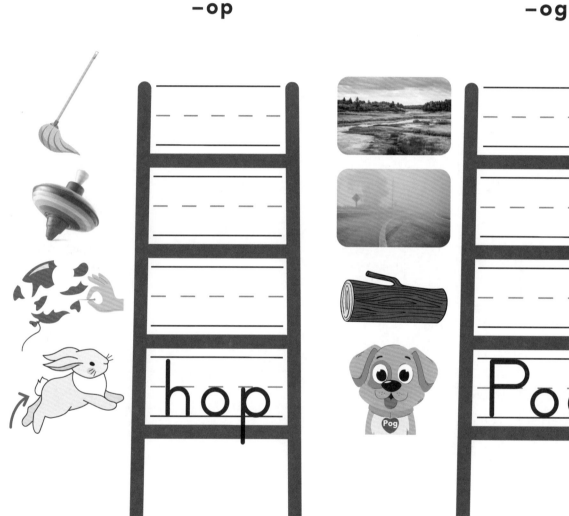

hop   Pog

Try This!

These are nonsense words: *fom*, *gom*, *som*. They all rhyme. What nonsense words can you make that rhyme with *hop*?

Name: _____ Date: _____

Directions: Read the story with a friend or adult. Use the words in the Word Bank to complete the story. Draw a picture to answer the question.

Word Bank

dog   hops   pit   Tom

Sam and Tom

_____

_ _ _ _ _ _ _

Sam is a _____.

_____

_ _ _ _ _ _ _

He walks by a _____.

_____

_ _ _ _ _ _ _

_____ sits in the pit.

_____

_ _ _ _ _ _ _

He _____ to see Sam.

What will happen next?

Short *Oo*

Name: _____ Date: _____

Directions: Trace the letters. Name each picture. Circle the letter for the sound you hear at the beginning of each word.

C c   L l

Consonants *Cc* and *Ll*

1.

c   l

6.

c   l

2.

c   l

7.

c   l

3.

c   l

8.

c   l

4.

c   l

9.

c   l

5.

c   l

10.

c   l

Directions: Trace the letters. Name the pictures. Circle the pictures that start with *c* or *l*. Follow the eggs to find the nest!

Cc   Ll

Name: _____ Date: _____

Directions: Name each picture. Say the beginning, middle, and ending sounds in each word. Write the missing letters in the boxes. Then, write the word.

1.

| | | b |

_ _ _ _ _ _ _

2.

| | | p |

_ _ _ _ _ _ _

3.

| p | a | |

_ _ _ _ _ _ _

4.

| l | | b |

_ _ _ _ _ _ _

5.

| | | t |

_ _ _ _ _ _ _

Try This!

Choose a word from above. Say each sound to a friend. Ask them to say the word. Then, switch roles.

Name: _____ Date: _____

Directions: Name each picture. Connect three letters to make the word. Write the word.

1.
   t   p
      o
   m   s
   _____
   - - - - - - - - -
   _____

2.
   l   b
      i
   n   t
   _____
   - - - - - - - - -
   _____

3.
   g   p
      o
   c   b
   _____
   - - - - - - - - -
   _____

4.
   c   n
      o
   t   g
   _____
   - - - - - - - - -
   _____

5.
   f   p
      i
   l   b
   _____
   - - - - - - - - -
   _____

6.
   c   p
      a
   d   s
   _____
   - - - - - - - - -
   _____

Consonants Cc and Ll

Directions: Write a sentence about Tom.

_____
- - - - - - - - - - - - - - - - - - -
_____

WEEK 14
DAY
5

Name: _____   Date: _____

Directions: Read the story with a friend or adult. Use the words in the Word Bank to complete the story. Draw a picture to answer the question.

Word Bank

jog   pal   tag   Tom

Consonants Cc and Ll

Tag

_____
— — — — — —

Tom is a _____ for Sam.

_____
— — — — — —

Tom says, "We can play _____."

_____
— — — — —

Tom and Sam _____ and jab.

_____
— — — — —

Sam got _____!

What will happen next?

84   130212—180 Days™: Phonics   © Shell Education

Name: _____ Date: _____

Directions: Trace the letters. Name the pictures. Draw a line to the letter you hear at the beginning of each word.

Directions: Draw something that starts with *h*. Then, draw something that starts with *j*.

Name: _____ Date: _____

Directions: Name the pictures. Listen to the beginning sound of each word. Circle the picture that has a different beginning sound in each row.

1.

2.

3.

4.

5.

Directions: Name each picture. Write the letter for the middle sound you hear in each word.

6.  ____   8.  ____

7.  ____   9.  ____

Consonants *Hh* and *Jj*

Name: _____ Date: _____

Directions: Touch each dot, and say the sound. Read the word. Then, draw a line from each word to the matching picture.

1. | h | o | t |
   ● ● ●

2. | j | o | b |
   ● ● ●

3. | h | i | p |
   ● ● ●

4. | J | i | m |
   ● ● ●

5. | h | i | t |
   ● ● ●

6. | j | i | g |
   ● ● ●

Consonants *Hh* and *Jj*

Name: _____ Date: _____

Directions: Name the pictures. Look for the words in the puzzle. Circle the words in the puzzle. Write the words on the lines. You may use letters more than once.

Consonants *Hh* and *Jj*

h	a	m	c	a	n
o	n	j	o	b	a
p	p	o	t	o	p

1. _____
   h___p

2. _____
   c_____

3. _____
   p_____

4. _____
   j_____

5. _____
   c___n

6. _____
   o___

7. _____
   n_____

8. _____
   h___m

9. _____
   t___p

Directions: Read the story with a friend or adult. Use the words in the Word Bank to complete the story. Draw a picture to go with the story.

Word Bank

hot	job	mop	stop

Jan's Job

_____

_ _ _ _ _ _ _

Jan has a _____.

_____

_ _ _ _ _ _ _

She starts to _____.

_____

_ _ _ _ _ _ _

But she has to _____.

_____

_ _ _ _ _ _

It is too _____!

Name: _____ Date: _____

Directions: Match each word to the picture that shows it.

cap

cat

cot

hip

hit

hot

jog

lap

lip

log

Name: _____ Date: _____

Directions: Name each picture. Write the letters you hear at the beginning and middle of each word.

c   l   h   j   o   a   i

1.  ___ ___ ___
___ ___ ___
___ ___p

2.  ___ ___ ___
___ ___ ___
___ ___g

3.  ___ ___ ___
___ ___ ___
___ ___b

4. ___ ___ ___
___ ___ ___
___ ___m

5.  ___ ___ ___
___ ___ ___
___ ___g

6.  ___ ___ ___
___ ___ ___
___ ___p

7. ___ ___ ___
___ ___ ___
___ ___t

8. ___ ___ ___
___ ___ ___
___ ___d

Try This!

Read each of the words below. Act out each word. Have a friend guess the words.

sip   sit   pop   jog

Name: _____ Date: _____

Directions: Touch each dot, and say the sound. Read the phrases. Then, draw lines from the phrases to the matching pictures.

1.

2.

3.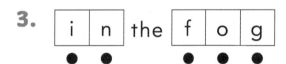

4.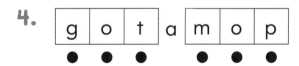

5.

Name: _____ Date: _____

Directions: Name the pictures. Read the word at the bottom of each ladder. Change the first letter in each word as you go up the ladder.

–ot

–ob

Name: _____ Date: _____

Directions: Read the story with a friend or adult. Use the words in the Word Bank to complete the story. Draw a picture to go with the story.

Word Bank

big   bug   hop   log

Ben the Bug

_____

– – – – – –

Ben is a _____.

_____

– – – – – –

He is not _____.

_____

– – – – – –

He sits on a _____.

_____

– – – – – –

He likes to _____.

Overview

Short Vowel *Uu* and Consonants *Rr, Kk, Dd,* and *Yy*

The /k/ sound can be spelled with the letter *k* and the letters *ck*. When the sound occurs at the beginning of a word, it is often spelled with the letter *k*, such as in *kite*, *kangaroo*, and *key*. When the /k/ sound follows a short vowel (often at the end of a word), it is spelled with a *ck*, such as in *rock*, *kick*, and *pack*.

In this unit, students will continue studying word families. They will also learn to recognize the /k/ sound and the two ways it can be spelled.

Directions: Look at the words. The *u* makes a short "uh" sound. Listen to each sound in the words. Repeat each sound in the words. Then, say the words normally.

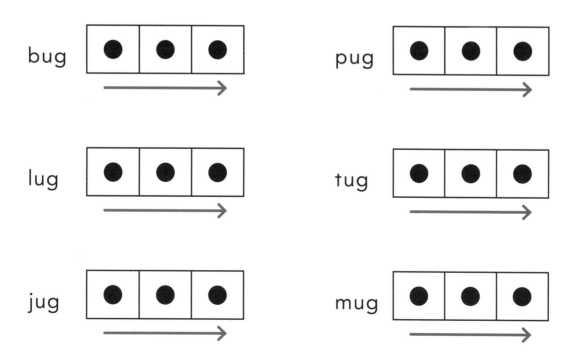

bug

pug

lug

tug

jug

mug

Name: _____   Date: _____

Directions: Trace the letters. Name the pictures. Circle the pictures that have the ŭ sound.

Directions: Read the sentence. Circle the words that have the ŭ sound. Draw a picture to go with the sentence.

Gus can run for fun.

Short Uu

Name: _____ Date: _____

Directions: Read the words on the rainbow. Use the key to color the picture.

rhymes with **fun** green	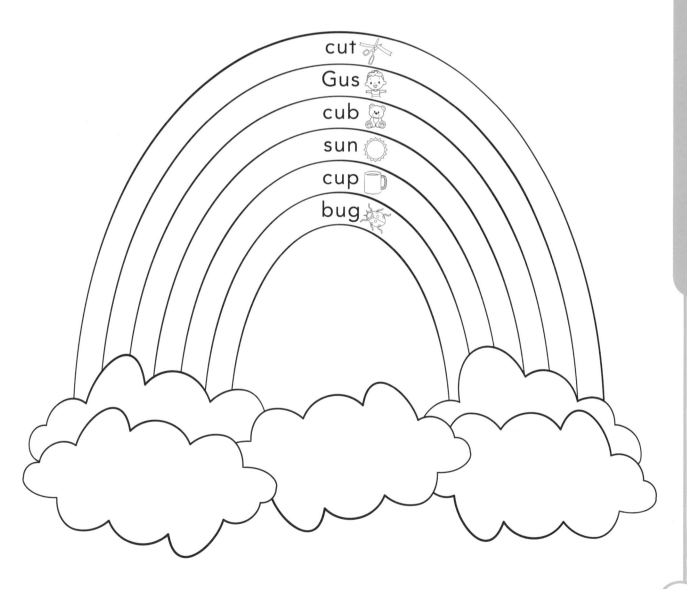	rhymes with **pup** blue	
rhymes with **hug** purple		rhymes with **hut** red	
rhymes with **bus** orange		rhymes with **sub** yellow	

cut
Gus
cub
sun
cup
bug

Name: _____   Date: _____

Directions: Name each picture. Say the beginning, middle, and ending sounds in each word. Write the missing letters in the boxes. Then, write the word.

1.

		m

_ _ _ _ _ _

2.

		b

_ _ _ _ _ _

3.

		g

_ _ _ _ _ _

4.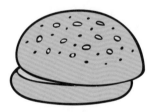

		n

_ _ _ _ _ _

5.

	u	g

_ _ _ _ _ _

6.

t		g

_ _ _ _ _ _

Name: _____ Date: _____

Directions: Name the pictures. Read the word at the bottom of each ladder. Change the beginning sound in each word as you go up the ladder.

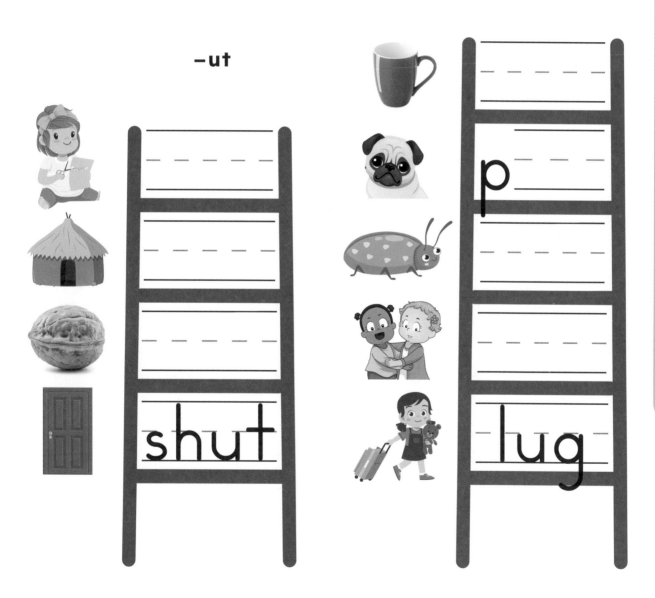

-ug

-ut

p

shut

lug

Name: _____   Date: _____

Directions: Read the story. Draw a picture for each sentence. Then, draw a picture to answer the question.

Pog the Pug

Pog is a pug. He is a pup.

Pog is at the park.

Pog is in the sun.

Pog is in the cab.

Where will Pog go?

Short Uu

Name: _____ Date: _____

Directions: Trace the letters. Name each picture. Then, write the letter you hear at the beginning of each word.

1.  ___ ___ ___   5.  ___ ___ ___

2.  ___ ___ ___   6.  ___ ___ ___

3.   ___ ___ ___   7.  ___ ___ ___

4.  ___ ___ ___   8.  ___ ___ ___

Consonants *Rr* and *Kk*

Directions: Draw something that starts with *r*. Then, draw something that starts with *k*.

Name: _____ Date: _____

Directions: Trace the letters. Name the pictures. Circle the pictures that begin with *k*.

K k

Directions: Trace the letters. Name the pictures. Circle the pictures that end with *ck*.

ck

Name: _____ Date: _____

Directions: Touch each dot, and say the sound. Read the word. Then, draw a line from each word to the matching picture.

1.

r	u	g

● ● ●

2.

R	i	ck

● ● ●

3.

r	a	m

● ● ●

4.

k	i	ck

● ● ●

5.

r	i	p

● ● ●

6.

l	u	ck

● ● ●

Consonants *Rr* and *Kk*

Name: _____   Date: _____

Directions: Name the pictures. Look for the words in the puzzle. Circle the words in the puzzle. Write the words on the lines. You may use letters more than once.

r	i	p	i	ck	l
a	r	a	t	o	ck
ck	u	ck	r	u	n

1. ___ __ __
   p____ck

3. ___ __ __
   p____ck

5. ___ __ __
   ____ip

2. ___ __ __
   r____t

4. ___ __ __
   r____ck

6. ___ __ __
   ru____

Directions: Read the tongue twisters with a friend or adult. Draw a picture for one tongue twister.

Tongue Twisters

Big Bob bit a bug by the bog.

Cam can cut a cup of carrots.

Pog the pug has a pig pal.

Tim tugs a tin tab to the tip.

Rick the rat ran to the rock rim.

Name: _____   Date: _____

Directions: Trace the letters. Name each picture. Circle the letter for the sound you hear at the beginning of each word.

Dd   Yy

1.   d   y   6.   d   y

2.   d   y   7.   d   y

3.   d   y   8.   d   y

4.   d   y   9.   d   y

5.   d   y   10.   d   y

Directions: Draw a picture to show each word.

dot [   ]   yum [   ]

Consonants *Dd* and *Yy*

Directions: Name each picture. Write the letter you hear at the beginning of each word.

1. __ __

2.  __ __

3.  __ __

4.  __ __

5.  __ __

6.  __ __

Directions: Name each picture. Write the letter you hear at the end of each word.

7.  __ __

8.  __ __

9.  __ __

10.  __ __

Consonants Dd and Yy

Name: _____ Date: _____

Directions: Touch each dot, and say the sound. Read the word. Then, draw a line from each word to the matching picture.

1.
y	u	ck

● ● ●

2.
d	u	ck

● ● ●

3.
k	i	d

● ● ●

4.
h	i	d

● ● ●

5.
d	o	ck

● ● ●

6.
y	u	m

● ● ●

Name: _____   Date: _____

Directions: Name the pictures. Read the word at the bottom of each ladder. Change the first letter in each word as you go up the ladder.

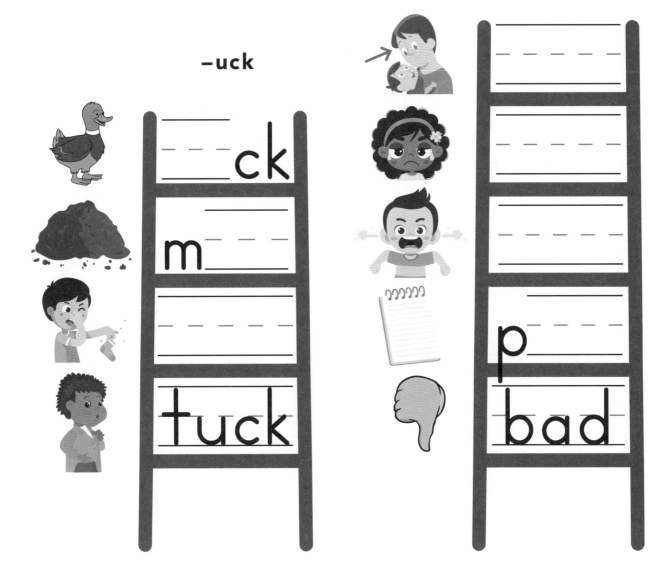

-ad

-uck

_____ck

m_____

_____

tuck

p_____

bad

Name: _____   Date: _____

Directions: Read the story with a friend or adult. Write words from the story to finish the sentences.

Consonants *Dd* and *Yy*

Pog and the Duck

Pog is a pug.

Jud is a duck.

Pog and Jud tug a red bug.

It is stuck in the muck!

It is bad luck!

Pog and Jud dig for the bug.

They say, "Yuck!"

_____
– – – – – – – –

1. Pog is a _____.

_____
– – – – – – – –

2. Jud is a _____.

_____
– – – – – – – –

3. A bug is in the _____.

_____
– – – – – – – –

4. Pog and Jud dig for the _____.

_____
– – – – – – – –

5. They say, "_____!"

Directions: Match each word to the picture that shows it.

duck

rock

lock

ram

rug

sad

dock

sun

yak

yuck

DAY 2

Name: _____ Date: _____

Directions: Name the pictures. Listen to the ending sound of each word. Circle the picture that has a different ending sound in each row.

Review: Uu, Rr, Kk, Dd, Yy

1.

2.

3.

4.

5.

Directions: Name the pictures. Write the letters for the beginning and middle sounds in each word.

6. ___ ___
___ ___ ___
___ ___ ck

8. ___ ___
___ ___ ___
___ ___ g

7.  ___ ___
___ ___ ___
___ ___ m

9.  ___ ___
___ ___ ___
___ ___ ck

130212—180 Days™: Phonics   © Shell Education

Name: _____ Date: _____

Directions: Name each picture. Write the words in the chart.

c	— — — – – – – — — —	— — — – – – – — — —
r	— — — – – – – ___ ___ck	— — — – – – – — — —
d	— — — – – – ___ ___ck	— — — – – – — — —
y	— — — – – – – — — —	— — — – – – – — — —

Name: _____ Date: _____

Directions: Name each picture. Say the beginning, middle, and ending sounds you hear in the word. Use the letters to write the word. Then, color the pictures.

1.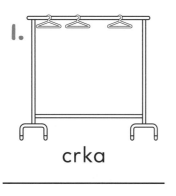

crka

_____

_ _ _ _ _ _ _

_____

4.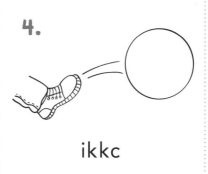

ikkc

_____

_ _ _ _ _ _ _

_____

7.

kcpu

_____

_ _ _ _ _ _ _

_____

2.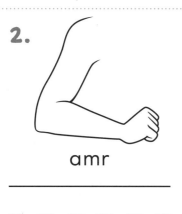

amr

_____

_ _ _ _ _ _ _

_____

5.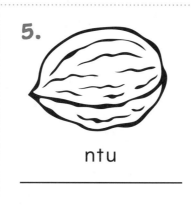

ntu

_____

_ _ _ _ _ _ _

_____

8.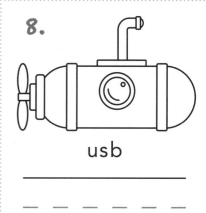

usb

_____

_ _ _ _ _ _ _

_____

3.

pyi

_____

_ _ _ _ _ _ _

_____

6.

idk

_____

_ _ _ _ _ _ _

_____

9.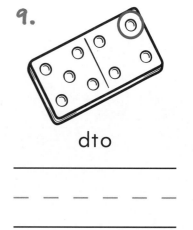

dto

_____

_ _ _ _ _ _ _

_____

Directions: Put two game markers on **Start**. Take turns rolling a number cube with a partner. Move your game marker the number of spaces you roll. Then, say the word you land on. Use it in a sentence. The first player to land on **End** wins.

End

sum	pick	nod	tug	hid	buck	run

		rot

Start

sick		sack
yum		sun
rug		yak

luck	dad	yap	fun	rag	dog	sock

Overview

Short Vowel *Ee* and Consonants *Qq, Ww, Vv, Xx,* and *Zz*

In this unit, students will continue learning about letters and the sounds they make. Students will learn the letter *q*, which is usually followed by the letter *u*. The sound that is represented by *qu* is /kw/, which is the blend of /k/ and /w/. Students will identify *q* and *u* together in this unit.

Directions: Look at the words. The *e* makes a short "eh" sound. Listen to each sound in the words. Repeat each sound in the words. Then, say the words normally. What word family do these words belong to?

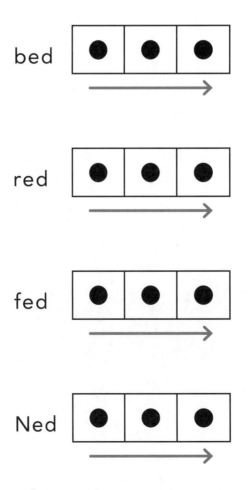

bed

red

fed

Ned

Directions: Trace the letters. Name the pictures. Circle the pictures that have the ĕ sound.

Directions: Draw something that has the ĕ sound in its name.

Name: _____ Date: _____

Directions: Name each picture. Write the letter you hear in the middle of each word.

1.  _____
   _ _ _
   _____

2.  _____
   _ _ _
   _____

3.  _____
   _ _ _
   _____

4.  _____
   _ _ _
   _____

5.  _____
   _ _ _
   _____

6.  _____
   _ _ _
   _____

7. 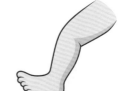 _____
   _ _ _
   _____

8.  _____
   _ _ _
   _____

Directions: Name each picture. Write the letter or letters you hear at the end of each word.

9.  _____
   _ _ _
   _____

10.  _____
    _ _ _
    _____

11. _____
    _ _ _
    _____

12.  _____
    _ _ _
    _____

Name: _____ Date: _____

Directions: Touch each dot, and say the sound. Read the word. Then, draw a line from each word to the matching picture.

1.

j	e	t

● ● ●

2.

n	e	ck

● ● ●

3.

w	e	d

● ● ●

4.

d	e	ck

● ● ●

5.

p	e	ck

● ● ●

6.

g	e	t

● ● ●

Short Ee

130212—180 Days™: Phonics

Name: _____ Date: _____

Directions: Name the pictures. Read the word at the bottom of each ladder. Change the first letter in each word as you go up the ladder.

Short Ee

–en

K_____

den

–ed

T_____

fed

Try This!

Choose a word from above. Tap each sound on your fingers while saying it. Then, snap your fingers, and say the word. Do this for four more words.

Name: _____ Date: _____

WEEK 21
DAY
5

Directions: Read the story with a friend or adult. Use the words in the Word Bank to complete the story. Then, answer the question.

Word Bank

led   met   sack   sat

Short Ee

Meg and Ren

_____

Meg _____ her friend, Ren.

Meg _____ Ren to the rock.

Ren had a _____.

They _____ on the rock.

What will Meg and Ren do?

_____

_____

_____

_____

© Shell Education   130212—180 Days™: Phonics   **121**

Name: _____ Date: _____

Directions: Trace the letters. Name each picture. Circle the letters you hear at the beginning of the words. The letters *q* and *u* work together to make the /qu/ sound.

Qq   Ww

1.    qu   w

2.    qu   w

3.    qu   w

4.    qu   w

5.    qu   w

6.    qu   w

7.    qu   w

8.    qu   w

9.    qu   w

10.    qu   w

Directions: Trace the letters. Name the pictures. Circle the soccer balls with pictures that start with *qu* or *w*. Follow the balls to find the goal!

Qq   Ww

Consonants Qq and Ww

Name: _____ Date: _____

Directions: Touch each dot, and say the sound. Read the word. Then, draw a line from each word to the matching picture.

1. | w | e | b |
● ● ●

2. | w | i | ck |
● ● ●

3. | qu | a | ck |
● ● ●

4. | w | a | g |
● ● ●

5. | qu | i | t |
● ● ●

6. | w | i | n |
● ● ●

quack

Try This!

Choose a word from above. Skywrite the word as you say each sound. Then, say the whole word. Do this for three more words.

Consonants Qq and Ww

Name: _____ Date: _____

Directions: Name each picture. Connect letters to make the word. Write the word.

1.

   w   n
        i
   r   t

   _____
   - - - - - - -
   _____

2.

   m   s
        i
   w   ck

   _____
   - - - - - - -
   _____

3.

   qu   p
        i
   ck   t

   _____
   - - - - - - -
   _____

4.

   t   ck
        a
   qu   v

   _____
   - - - - - - -
   _____

5.

   w   p
        i
   c   g

   _____
   - - - - - - -
   _____

6.

   w   b
        e
   g   t

   _____
   - - - - - - -
   _____

Directions: Write a sentence about an animal that is quick.

_____

- - - - - - - - - - - - - - - - - - -

_____

Name: _____   Date: _____

Directions: Read the letter with a friend or adult. Use the words in the Word Bank to complete the story.

Consonants Qq and Ww

Word Bank

duck   fed   Meg   quack   rock

_____
- - - - - - - - - -
Dear _____,
_____
- - - - - - - - - -
I am by a big _____.
_____
- - - - - - - - - -
I saw a _____.
_____
- - - - - - - - - -
I _____ the duck.
_____
- - - - - - - - - -
It said, "_____!"

Love, Ren

Directions: Write a sentence about Ren.

_____
- -
_____

Name: _____ Date: _____

Directions: Trace the letters. Name the pictures. Draw a line to the letter you hear at the beginning of each word.

Directions: Trace the letters. Name the pictures. Circle the pictures that end with *x*.

Consonants Vv, Xx, and Zz

Name: _____ Date: _____

Consonants Vv, Xx, and Zz

Directions: Name the pictures. Listen to the beginning sound in each word. Circle the picture that has a different beginning sound in each row.

1.

2.

3.

4.

Directions: Name the pictures. Listen to the ending sound in each word. Circle the picture that has a different ending sound in each row.

5.

6.

7.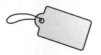

8.

Directions: Name each picture. Say the beginning, middle, and ending sounds in each word. Write the letters in the boxes. Then, write the word.

1.

t	u	

_ _ _ _ _ _

2.

_ _ _ _ _ _

3.

_ _ _ _ _ _

4.

f	i	

_ _ _ _ _ _

5.

_ _ _ _ _ _

Consonants Vv, Xx, and Zz

Name: _____   Date: _____

Directions: Name the pictures. Read the word at the bottom of each ladder. Change the first letter in each word as you go up the ladder.

–et

–ix

pet

6

six

....

Directions: Write a sentence using one of the words above. Circle the word in your sentence.

_____

_ _

_____

Name: _____ Date: _____

Directions: Read the story with a friend or adult. Write words from the story to finish the sentences.

Liz and Rex

Liz is a fox.

Rex has a tux.

Liz and Rex can mix.

They fix a quick mix from a box.

They fix six cookies for the vet.

1. Liz is a _____.

2. Rex has a _____.

3. They fix a quick _____.

4. They fix six cookies for the _____.

Directions: Draw your favorite cookie. Label the picture.

Name: _____ Date: _____

Directions: Match each word to the picture that shows it.

box

fox

mix

quack

six

tux

vet

wag

wig

zip

Name: _____ Date: _____

Directions: Name each picture. Write the missing letters.
Note: *qu* is one sound.

qu   w   v   x   z   i   o   u

1.    ___ ___ ___

    ___ ___ ___ ___

    ___ ___ ___p

2.    ___ ___ ___

    ___ ___ ___ ___

    ___ e ___

3.    ___ ___ ___

    ___ ___ ___ ___

    ___ ___ ___

4. 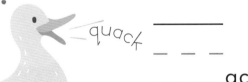   ___ ___

    ___ ___ ___ ___

    ___ack

5.   ___ ___ ___

    ___ ___ ___ ___

    ___ ___ ___

6.    ___ ___ ___

    ___ ___ ___ ___

    fi ___ ___

7.    ___ ___ ___

    ___ ___ ___ ___

    ___ ___ ___

8.   ___ ___ ___

    ___ ___ ___ ___

    ___ ___ ___

Review: Ee, Qq, Vv, Ww, Xx, Zz

Try This!

Write the words above in sidewalk chalk.
Walk, hop, or skip along the letters. Say the
sounds as you go. Then, say the whole word.

Name: _____ Date: _____

Directions: Touch each dot, and say the sound. Read the word. Then, draw a line from each word to the matching picture.

1.
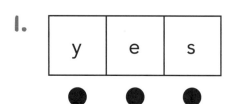

2.
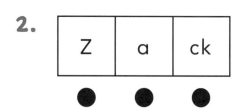

3.
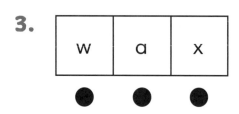

4.
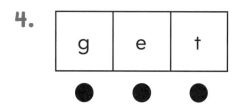

5.
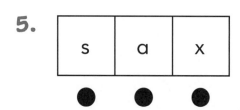

6.
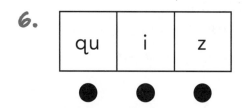

Name: _____ Date: _____

Directions: Name each picture. Say the beginning, middle, and ending sounds you hear in the word. Use the letters to write the word. Then, color the pictures.

1.

sye

_____
- - - - - - - - - - -
_____

4.

imx

_____
- - - - - - - - - - -
_____

7.

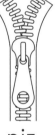

xof

_____
- - - - - - - - - - -
_____

2.

piz

_____
- - - - - - - - - - -
_____

5.

bew

_____
- - - - - - - - - - -
_____

8.

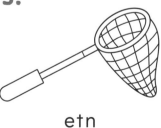

nep

_____
- - - - - - - - - - -
_____

3.

etn

_____
- - - - - - - - - - -
_____

6.

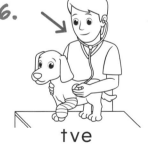

tve

_____
- - - - - - - - - - -
_____

9.

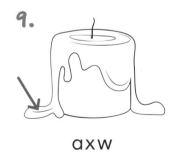

axw

_____
- - - - - - - - - - -
_____

Name: _____ Date: _____

Directions: Look at the pictures. Use the words to write sentences that match the pictures. Then, read the sentences aloud. **Note:** A sentence starts with a capital letter. A name starts with a capital letter.

1.

a	pet!	got	Max

_____

- - - - - - - - - - - - - - - - - - -

_____

2.

name	Wen.	is	Her

_____

- - - - - - - - - - - - - - - - - - -

_____

3.

quick!	is	Wen

_____

- - - - - - - - - - - - - - - - - - -

_____

4.

Wen!	mix	Max	treats	can	for

_____

- - - - - - - - - - - - - - - - - - -

_____

- - - - - - - - - - - - - - - - - - -

_____

Overview

CVC Words

Now that students have practiced recognizing all 26 letters and their sounds, they can begin putting them together in simple words. CVC (consonant-vowel-consonant) words are some of the simplest. These three-letter words use regular sound-spelling patterns and have short vowels, making them ideal for early reading practice. In this unit, students will read and write CVC words.

Directions: Look at the words. Listen to each sound in the words. Repeat each sound in the words. Then, say the words normally.

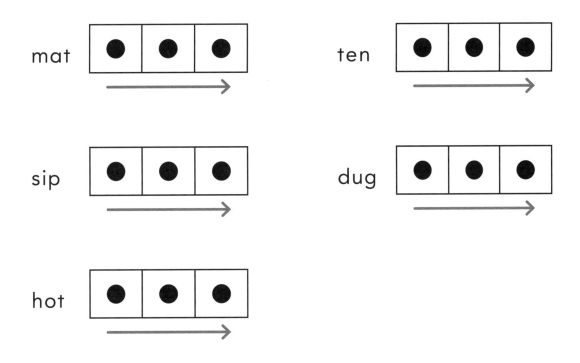

mat

ten

sip

dug

hot

Name: _____   Date: _____

Directions: Name each picture. Write short *a* words to make the sentences match the pictures. Color the pictures.

Short Aa Words

_____
– – – – – – – – – – – – –

1. He has a _____.

_____
– – – – – – – – – – – – –

2. The dog can _____.

_____
– – – – – – – – – – – – –

3. Jack is _____.

_____
– – – – – – – – – – – – –

4. Cam _____ to
_____
– – – – – – – – – – – – –
the _____.

Directions: Write the beginning and ending sounds for each picture.

5.  ____ ____
          – – – – – – –
          ____ a ____

7. 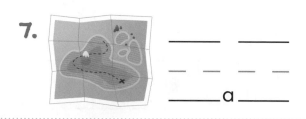 ____ ____
          – – – – – – –
          ____ a ____

6. 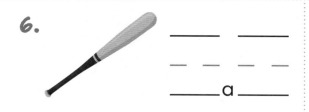 ____ ____
          – – – – – – –
          ____ a ____

8.  ____ ____
          – – – – – – –
          ____ a ____

Directions: Read the word endings. Name each picture.
Write the word ending you hear in each word.

an	at	ag	am	ab	ack	ad	ap

1.

f ☐

5.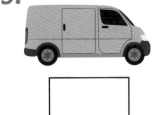

v ☐

9.

d ☐

2.

l ☐

6.

l ☐

10.

j ☐

3.

r ☐

7.

t ☐

11.

c ☐

4.

r ☐

8.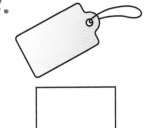

t ☐

12.

b ☐

Name: _____   Date: _____

Directions: Name each short *a* word. Write the letters you hear. Draw a line from each word to the one it rhymes with. **Note:** *Qu* and *ck* each make one sound.

1.
    ___ ___ ___
    - - - - - -
    ___ ___ ___

    ___ ___ ___
    - - - - - -
    ___ ___ ___

2.
    ___ ___ ___
    - - - - - -
    ___ ___ ___

    ___ ___ ___
    - - - - - -
    ___ ___ ___

3.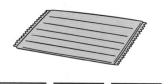
    ___ ___ ___
    - - - - - -
    ___ ___ ___

    ___ ___ ___
    - - - - - -
    s ___ ___

4.
    ___ ___ ___
    - - - - - -
    ___ ___ ___

    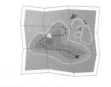
    ___ ___ ___
    - - - - - -
    ___ ___ ___

5.
    ___ ___ ___
    - - - - - -
    g ___ ___

    ___ ___ ___
    - - - - - -
    ___ ___ ___

Name: _____ Date: _____

Directions: Use the letters in the box to make words with the ă sound. Write the words on the lines. All words need to have one vowel sound.

 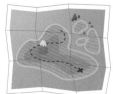 

p   t   b   m   a   g   ck   s   c

_____   _____

_ _ _ _ _ _ _ _ _ _ _ _ _   _ _ _ _ _ _ _ _ _ _ _ _ _

_____   _____

_____   _____

_ _ _ _ _ _ _ _ _ _ _ _ _   _ _ _ _ _ _ _ _ _ _ _ _ _

_____   _____

_____   _____

_ _ _ _ _ _ _ _ _ _ _ _ _   _ _ _ _ _ _ _ _ _ _ _ _ _

_____   _____

_____   _____

_ _ _ _ _ _ _ _ _ _ _ _ _   _ _ _ _ _ _ _ _ _ _ _ _ _

_____   _____

Name: _____ Date: _____

Directions: Circle the words that match each picture.

1.    big ram   big jab

2.    mad bat   mad cat

3.    bad van   bad cab

4.    sad yak   sad rat

5.    tan hat   tan fan

Directions: Write a sentence about one of the pictures above.

_____

_____

_____

_____

Name: _____   Date: _____

Directions: Name each picture. Write short *i* words to make the sentences match the pictures. Color the pictures.

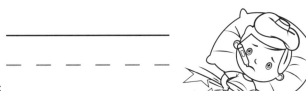

_____

‐ ‐ ‐ ‐ ‐ ‐ ‐ ‐ ‐ ‐ ‐ ‐ ‐

1. Rick b_____ the fig.

_____

‐ ‐ ‐ ‐ ‐ ‐ ‐ ‐ ‐ ‐ ‐ ‐ ‐

2. The kid is s_____.

_____

‐ ‐ ‐ ‐ ‐ ‐ ‐ ‐ ‐ ‐ ‐ ‐ ‐

3. She can _____!

_____

‐ ‐ ‐ ‐ ‐ ‐ ‐ ‐ ‐ ‐ ‐ ‐ ‐

4. I lit the w_____.

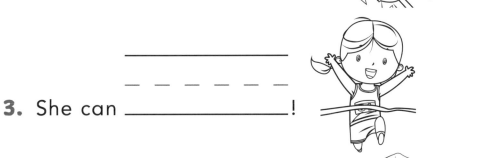

Short *Ii* Words

....

Directions: Write the beginning and ending sounds for each picture.

5. ___ ___

‐ ‐ ‐ ‐ ‐ ‐ ‐ ‐ ‐

___ i ___

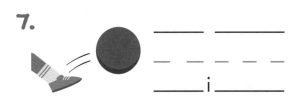
7. ___ ___

‐ ‐ ‐ ‐ ‐ ‐ ‐ ‐ ‐

___ i ___

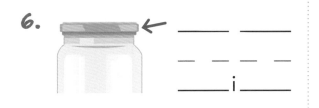
6. ___ ___

‐ ‐ ‐ ‐ ‐ ‐ ‐ ‐ ‐

___ i ___

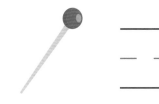
8. ___ ___

‐ ‐ ‐ ‐ ‐ ‐ ‐ ‐ ‐

___ i ___

Name: _____   Date: _____

Directions: Read the word endings. Name each picture. Write the word ending you hear in each word.

| in | it | ig | ick | id | ip | ix |

1.
p

2.
b

3.
s

4.
z

5.
l

6.
m

7.
k

8.
p

9.
r

10.
l

11.
f

12.
s

Name: _____ Date: _____

Directions: Name each short *i* word. Write the letters you hear. Draw a line from each word to the one it rhymes with. **Note:** *Ck* makes one sound.

1.
   ____ ____

   p____ ____

   r____ m

2.
   ____ ____ ____

   ____ ____ ____

3.
   ____ ____

   s____ ____

   ____ ____ ____

4.
   ____ ____

   K____ ____

   ____ ____ ____

5.
   ____ ____

   ____ ____ ____

© Shell Education

Short *Ii* Words

Name: _____ Date: _____

Directions: Use the letters in the box to make words with the ĭ sound. Write the words on the lines. All words need to have one vowel sound.

Short *Ii* Words

s   ck   t   b   i   g   k   p

_____   _____

- - - - - - - - - -   - - - - - - - - - -

_____   _____

- - - - - - - - - -   - - - - - - - - - -

_____   _____

_____   _____

- - - - - - - - - -   - - - - - - - - - -

_____   _____

- - - - - - - - - -   - - - - - - - - - -

_____   _____

Try This!

Write the word parts below on cards. Use them to make as many words as you can. Then, use the words in sentences.

at, ot, en, ig, b, h, m, p, r, t

Directions: Circle the words that match each picture.

1.    Liz can tip.   Liz can sit.

2.    Ben can hit.   Ben can dip.

3.    Gus can rip.   Gus can sip.

4.    Mel can lick.   Mel can win.

5.    Deb can pick.   Deb can kick.

Short Ii Words

Directions: Write a sentence about what you can do.

_____

_____

_____

_____

Name: _____   Date: _____

Directions: Name each picture. Write short *o* words to make the sentences match the pictures. Color the pictures.

_____

– – – – – – – –

1. She sat on the _____.

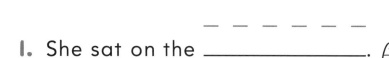
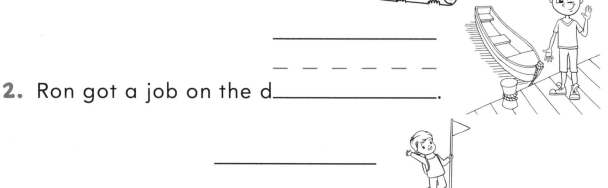

_____

– – – – – – – –

2. Ron got a job on the d_____.

_____

– – – – – – – –

3. I went to the tip-_____.

_____

– – – – – – – –

4. He likes to _____.

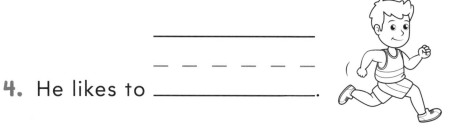

....

Directions: Write the beginning and ending sounds for each picture.

5.  ____ ____
   – – – – – –
   ____ o ____

7. 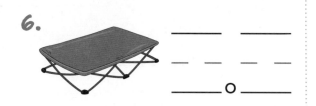 ____ ____
   – – – – – –
   ____ o ____

6.  ____ ____
   – – – – – –
   ____ o ____

8. 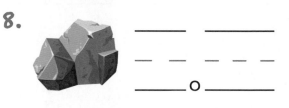 ____ ____
   – – – – – –
   ____ o ____

Name: _____ Date: _____

Directions: Read the word endings. Name each picture. Write the word ending you hear in each word.

om	ot	og	ock	ob	op	ox

1.

l____

2.

m____

3.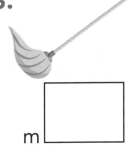

m____

4.

s____

5.

b____

6.

h____

7.

p____

8.

h____

9.

d____

10.

s____

11.

c____

12.

f____

Short *Oo* Words

Name: _____   Date: _____

Directions: Name each short *o* word. Write the letters you hear. Draw a line from each word to the one it rhymes with. **Note:** *Ck* makes one sound.

Short *Oo* Words

1.

   ___ ___ ___

   ___ ___ ___

   ___ ___ ___

   ___ ___ ___

   ___ ___ ___

   ___ ___ ___

2.

   ___ ___ ___

   ___ ___ ___

   ___ ___ ___

   ___ ___ ___

   ___ ___ ___

   ___ ___ ___

3.

   ___ ___ ___

   ___ ___ ___

   ___ ___t

   ___ ___ ___

   ___ ___ ___

   ___ ___ ___

4.

   ___ ___ ___

   ___ ___ ___

   ___ ___ ___

   ___ ___ ___

   ___ ___ ___

   ___ ___ ___

5.

   ___ ___ ___

   ___ ___ ___

   j___ ___

   ___ ___ ___

   ___ ___ ___

   ___ ___ ___

Directions: Use the letters in the box to make words with the ŏ sound. Write the words on the lines. All words need to have one vowel sound.

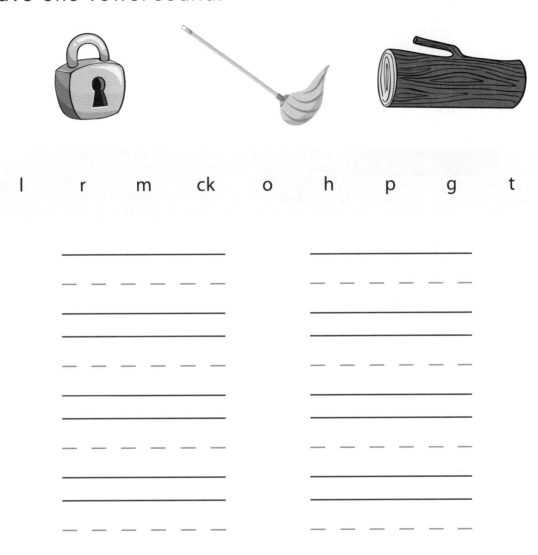

l   r   m   ck   o   h   p   g   t

_____   _____

_ _ _ _ _ _ _ _ _ _ _   _ _ _ _ _ _ _ _ _ _ _

_____   _____

_____   _____

_ _ _ _ _ _ _ _ _ _ _   _ _ _ _ _ _ _ _ _ _ _

_____   _____

_____   _____

_ _ _ _ _ _ _ _ _ _ _   _ _ _ _ _ _ _ _ _ _ _

_____   _____

_____   _____

_ _ _ _ _ _ _ _ _ _ _   _ _ _ _ _ _ _ _ _ _ _

_____   _____

Short *Oo* Words

Try This!

Ask an adult to write short words in pen or marker. Use watercolor to paint over the letters. Say each sound, and blend the words.

Name: _____ Date: _____

Directions: Circle the words that match each picture.

1.    big rock   big sock

2.    tan hog   tan log

3.    top cot   top hot

4.    fun fox   fun mom

5.    wet jog   wet cog

Directions: Write a sentence about one of the pictures from this page.

_____

_____

_____

_____

Name: _____ Date: _____

Directions: Name each picture. Write short *u* words to make the sentences match the pictures. Color the pictures.

_____
- - - - - - - - -

1. Gus had some _____.

_____
- - - - - - - - -

2. A cub sits in the _____.

_____
- - - - - - - - -

3. Jud gets on the _____.

_____
- - - - - - - - -

4. The p_____ is in

_____
- - - - - - - - -

the _____!

· ·

Directions: Write the beginning and ending sounds for each picture.

5. 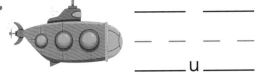 _____ _____
- - - - - - -
____ u ____

7.  _____ _____
- - - - - - -
____ u ____

6.  _____ _____
- - - - - - -
____ u ____

8. _____ _____
- - - - - - -
____ u ____

Name: _____ Date: _____

Directions: Read the word endings. Name each picture. Write the word ending you hear in each word.

ut	ug	uck	ub	up	un	us

Short Uu Words

1.
t ☐

5.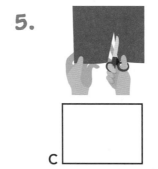
c ☐

9.
b ☐

2.
d ☐

6.
y ☐

10.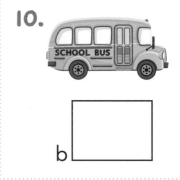
b ☐

3.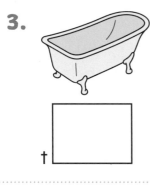
t ☐

7.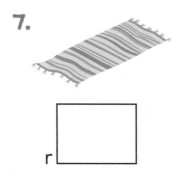
r ☐

11.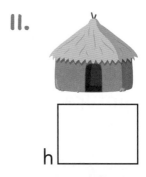
h ☐

4.
s ☐

8.
p ☐

12.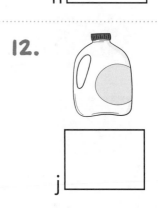
j ☐

Directions: Name each short *u* word. Write the letters you hear. Draw a line from each word to the one it rhymes with. **Note:** *Ck* makes one sound.

1.

____ ____ ____ ____

- - - - - - - -

____ ____ ____ ____

____ ____ ____ ____

- - - - - - - -

____ ____ ____ ____

2.

____ ____ ____ ____

- - - - - - - -

l____ ____ ____

____ ____ ____ ____

- - - - - - - -

____ ____n

3.

____ ____ ____ ____

- - - - - - - -

____ ____ ____ ____

____ ____ ____

- - - - - - - -

____ ____p

4.

____ ____ ____

- - - - - -

____ ____g

____ ____ ____

- - - - - -

c____ ____

5.

____ ____ ____

- - - - - -

____ ____ ____

____ ____ ____ ____

- - - - - - - -

____ ____ ____ ____

Short *Uu* Words

Name: _____ Date: _____

Directions: Use the letters in the box to make words with the ŭ sound. Write the words on the lines. All words need to have one vowel sound.

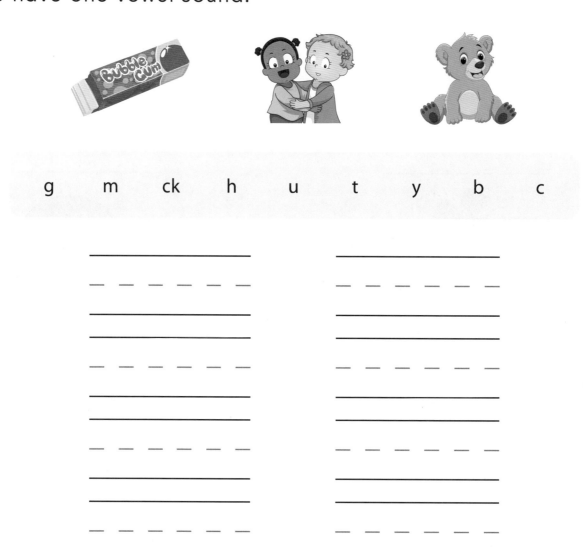

g   m   ck   h   u   t   y   b   c

_____   _____

_____   _____

_____   _____

_____   _____

_____   _____

Try This!

Choose three words from above. Hop while saying each sound. Then, do a big jump while saying the whole word.

Directions: Circle the words that match each picture.

1.

   Dan can run.   Dan can rub.

2.

   Tom can lug.   Tom can cut.

3.

   Kim can tug.   Kim can hug.

4.

   Gus can sit in   Gus can sit in
   the tub.   the sun.

5.

   Pam can have   Pam can have
   fun.   fur.

Directions: Write a new sentence about what a dog can do.

_____

_ _ _ _ _ _ _ _ _ _ _ _ _ _ _

_____

_ _ _ _ _ _ _ _ _ _ _ _ _ _ _

_____

Short Uu Words

Name: _____   Date: _____

Directions: Name each picture. Write short *e* words to make the sentences match the pictures. Color the pictures.

_____

_ _ _ _ _ _ _ _ _ _

1. Jen is on her _____.

_____

_ _ _ _ _ _ _ _ _ _

2. He _____ the cat.

_____

_ _ _ _ _ _ _ _ _ _

3. The dog will get _____!

_____

_ _ _ _ _ _ _ _ _ _

4. She hurt her _____.

Directions: Write the beginning and ending sounds for each picture.

5.  ____ ____
_ _ _ _ _ _ _
____ e ____

7.  ____ ____
_ _ _ _ _ _ _
____ e ____

6.   ____ ____
_ _ _ _ _ _ _
____ e ____

8. 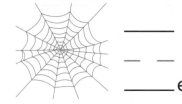 ____ ____
_ _ _ _ _ _ _
____ e ____

Directions: Read the word endings. Name each picture. Write the word ending you hear in each word.

et	en	eg	eb	eck	ed

1.
w [ ]

5.
m [ ]

9.
n [ ]

2.
b [ ]

6.
l [ ]

10.
b [ ]

3.
w [ ]

7.
p [ ]

11.
h [ ]

4.
p [ ]

8.
p [ ]

12.
j [ ]

Short Ee Words

Name: _____   Date: _____

Directions: Name each short *e* word. Write the letters you hear. Draw a line from each word to the one it rhymes with. **Note:** *Ck* makes one sound.

1.

____ ____ ____   ____ ____ ____

2.

____ ____ ____   ____ ____n

3.

____ ____ ____   ____ ____ ____

4.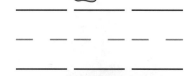

____ ____ ____   ____ ____ ____

5.

M____ ____   ____ ____ ____

Name: _____   Date: _____

Directions: Use the letters in the box to make words with the ĕ sound. Write the words on the lines. All words need to have one vowel sound.

v   d   n   p   e   w   ck   t   b

_____   _____

_____   _____

_____   _____

_____   _____

_____   _____

_____   _____

_____   _____

_____   _____

_____   _____

Name: _____ Date: _____

Directions: Circle the words that match each picture.

1.

      red pet   red pen

2.

      hot mug   hot bug

3.

      big deck   big neck

4.

      tan leg   tan bed

5.

      red jet   red men

Directions: Write a sentence about what Meg has. Use words from this page.

_____

- - - - - - - - - - - - - - - - - -

_____

_____

- - - - - - - - - - - - - - - - - -

_____

Short Ee Words

Name: _____ Date: _____

Directions: Name the pictures in the color key. Find the words that start with the same sounds. Use the key to color those squares.

red	blue	green	orange

yellow	purple	pink

buck	fit	Deb	set	fed	Peg
pen	sack	bid	mad	dab	did
fib	tack	pick	sob	tot	mix
mop	fix	pad	tick	bed	tax

Name: _____   Date: _____

Directions: Name each picture. Write the vowel you hear in each word.

a   e   i   o   u

1.

h___t

5.

p___ck

2.

w___g

6.

t___x

3.

d___g

7.

p___ck

4.

j___g

8.

c___b

Name: _____ Date: _____

Directions: Name each picture. Circle the letters you hear in each word. Blend the sounds, and write the word. Color the pictures. The first one has been done for you.

Say	Sounds			Write
	t (f)	(a) u	m (n)	_fan_
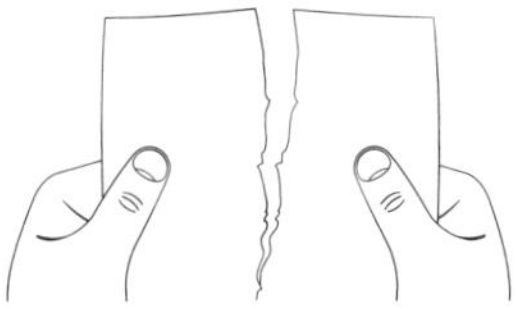	r v	e i	b p	
	c qu	i u	t ck	
	m n	o u	d j	
	d g	a i	g f	
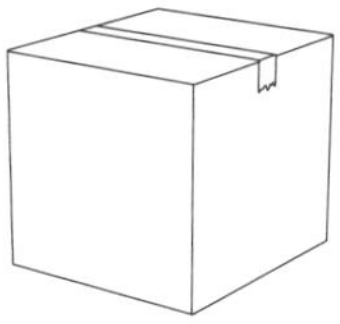	b f	o a	z x	
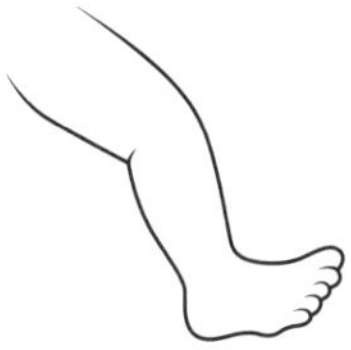	t l	u e	j g	
	h y	e a	m r	

Review: CVC Words

© Shell Education

130212—180 Days™: Phonics

165

Name: _____ Date: _____

Directions: Name each picture. Write the missing letters to make the words.

1.

d _____ _____

2.

_____ _____ t

3.

ki _____ _____

4.

_____ u _____

5.

h _____ _____

6.

_____ _____ g

7.

_____ _____ n

8.

y _____ _____

9.
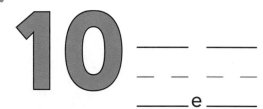
_____ e _____

10.

r _____ _____

Name: _____ Date: _____

Directions: Look at the pictures. Use the words to write sentences that match the pictures. Then, read the sentences aloud. **Note:** A sentence starts with a capital letter. A name starts with a capital letter.

1.

in	What	box?	is	the

_____

- - - - - - - - - - - - - - - -

_____

2.

can	Ron	tip	it.

_____

- - - - - - - - - - - - - - - -

_____

3.

mom	the	Ron's	box.	can	cut

_____

- - - - - - - - - - - - - - - -

_____

_____

4.

it!	hug	can	Ron

_____

- - - - - - - - - - - - - - - -

_____

Overview

Long Vowels *Aa*, *Ee*, *Ii*, *Oo*, and *Uu*

Vowels are letters that represent sounds made when air flows freely while speaking. Each vowel can have a short sound and a long sound. In this unit, words with long vowels are introduced with silent *e* and the *ee* vowel team.

Directions: Read each word on the left. Point to the vowel. Listen to each word on the right. Notice how the vowel sounds change. The *e* at the end of each word on the right is silent. But it makes the other vowels say their names.

cap	cape
pet	Pete
bit	bite
cop	cope
tub	tube

Name: _____ Date: _____

Directions: Read each word. Add a silent *e* to the end of each word. Write the new word. Then, draw a line from the words to the matching pictures.

_____
– – – – – – – –
1. cap + e = _____

_____
– – – – – – – –
2. tap + e = _____

_____
– – – – – – – –
3. can + e = _____

_____
– – – – – – – –
4. man + e = _____

_____
– – – – – – – –
5. bit + e = _____

_____
– – – – – – – –
6. dim + e = _____

_____
– – – – – – – –
7. kit + e = _____

_____
– – – – – – – –
8. rid + e = _____

Name: _____ Date: _____

Directions: Name each picture. Circle the long vowel sound you hear in each word.

a   i   a   i   a   i

a   i   a   i   a   i

a   i   a   i   a   i

Directions: Name each picture. Circle whether each vowel sound is long or short.

	long / short		long / short
	long / short		long / short

Name: _____ Date: _____

WEEK 31 DAY 3

Directions: Name each silent *e* word. Write the letters you hear. Write the silent *e*. Then, write the whole word. The first one has been done for you.

1.

| r | a | k | e rake

2.

3.

4.

5.

6.

Long Aa and Long Ii

© Shell Education   130212—180 Days™: Phonics   171

Name: _____ Date: _____

Directions: Name each picture of a silent *e* word. Write the missing letters to make the word. Then, write the whole word.

1.

   h ___ v ___   _____

2.

   c ___ v ___   _____

3.

   p ___ p ___   _____

4.

   h ___ d ___   _____

5.

   c ___ n ___   _____

6.

   b ___ t ___   _____

7.

   m ___ z ___   _____

130212—180 Days™: Phonics

Name: _____ Date: _____

Directions: Read the silent *e* words. Read the story with a friend or adult. Circle the rhyming words in the story.

| bite | Jake | kite | like | lime | ride | take | time |

Jake and Jack

Jake and Jack fly a kite.

Jake and Jack take a bite.

Jake and Jack ride the bus.

Jake and Jack are like us.

Jake and Jack pick a lime.

Jake and Jack like a good time!

Directions: Answer the question.

What else might Jake and Jack like to do?

_____

— — — — — — — — — — — — — — — — — — — —

_____

— — — — — — — — — — — — — — — — — — — —

_____

Name: _____ Date: _____

Directions: Read each word. Add a silent *e* to the end of each word. Write the new word. Then, draw a line from the words to the matching pictures.

_____

_ _ _ _ _ _

1. not + e = _____

_____

_ _ _ _ _ _

2. rob + e = _____

_____

_ _ _ _ _ _

3. rod + e = _____

_____

_ _ _ _ _ _

4. con + e = _____

_____

_ _ _ _ _ _

5. lob + e = _____

_____

_ _ _ _ _ _

6. wok + e = _____

_____

_ _ _ _ _ _

7. cod + e = _____

 130212—180 Days™: Phonics

Directions: Add the vowel team *ee* to the middle of each word. Write the new word. Then, draw a line from the words to the matching pictures.

1. m + _____ + t = _____

2. b + _____ + t = _____

3. w + _____ + d = _____

4. t + _____ + n = _____

5. f + _____ + t = _____

6. qu + _____ + n = _____

7. s + _____ + d = _____

8. p + _____ + l = _____

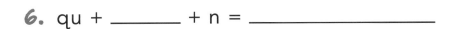

Name: _____   Date: _____

Directions: Name each word. Write the letters you hear in the boxes. Write the silent *e*. Then, write the whole word. The first one has been done for you.

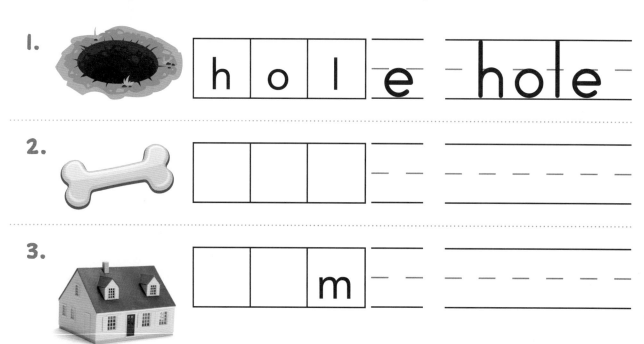

1. | h | o | l | e | hole

2. | | | | | _ _ _ _ _

3. | | | m | | _ _ _ _ _

Directions: Name each word. Write the letters you hear in the boxes. Then, write the word. The first one has been done for you.

4. | l | ee | k | leek

5. | | | | _ _ _ _ _

6. | | | | _ _ _ _ _

Long *Ee* and Long *Oo*

Directions: Name each picture. Use the letters to write the word.

♪	t e n o	_____
(cone)	n e o c	_____
(QR code)	c d e o	_____
(knot)	o p e r	_____

Directions: Name the pictures. Read the word at the bottom of each ladder. Change the first letter in each word as you go up the ladder.

meet

feed

Name: _____ Date: _____

Directions: Read the story with a friend or adult. Use the words in the Word Bank to complete the story.

Word Bank

deep   hole   home   made   peek

Long *Ee* and Long *Oo*

Pete's Home

_____

Pete has a big _____.

_____

We can take a _____!

_____

It is not a _____.

_____

It is _____.

_____

Pete _____ it.

It is a dam!

© Shell Education

Name: _____ Date: _____

Directions: Read each word. Add a silent *e* to the end of each word. Write the new word. Then, draw a line from the words to the matching pictures.

_____
— — — — — —
1. tub + e = _____

_____
— — — — — —
2. cut + e = _____

_____
— — — — — —
3. cub + e = _____

_____
— — — — — —
4. Jun + e = _____

_____
— — — — — —
5. dun + e = _____

_____
— — — — — —
6. tun + e = _____

_____
— — — — — —
7. mul + e = _____

_____
— — — — — —
8. rul + e = _____

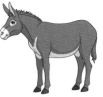

Long *Uu*

130212—180 Days™: Phonics

Name: _____ Date: _____

Directions: Name each picture. Circle whether each vowel sound is long or short.

Long Uu

1.

long   short

5.

long   short

2.

long   short

6.

long   short

3.

long   short

7.

long   short

4.

long   short

8.

long   short

Directions: Write a sentence about something that is cute.

_____

_ _

_____

Name: _____ Date: _____

Directions: Name each picture. Write a silent *e* at the end of each word. Touch each dot, and say the sound. Read the whole word. Then, write the word.

1.

m	u	l

● ● ●

_ _ _ _ _ _ _

2.

J	u	n

● ● ●

_ _ _ _ _ _ _

3.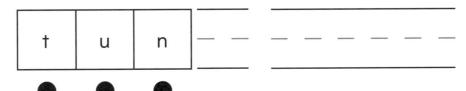

t	u	n

● ● ●

_ _ _ _ _ _ _

4.

c	u	b

● ● ●

_ _ _ _ _ _ _

5.

t	u	b

● ● ●

_ _ _ _ _ _ _

6.

c	u	t

● ● ●

_ _ _ _ _ _ _

Long *Uu*

Name: _____   Date: _____

Directions: Roll a number cube. Write the word ending for the number you rolled on the line. If you roll a six, choose one of the five endings. If the word you made is at the bottom of the page, circle it.

•	• •	• • •	• • • •	• • • • •	• • • • • •
ube	ute	une	ule	uke	You Choose

Long Uu

1. _____
   - - - - - - - - -
   r_____

4. _____
   - - - - - - - - -
   t_____

2. _____
   - - - - - - - - -
   c_____

5. _____
   - - - - - - - - -
   d_____

3. _____
   - - - - - - - - -
   m_____

6. _____
   - - - - - - - - -
   J_____

cube	cute	duke
dune	June	mule
rule	tube	tune

Name: _____ Date: _____

Directions: Read the story. Write words from the story to finish the sentences.

In June

In June, I cut a cute cake.

In June, I hum a fab tune.

In June, I ride a tan mule.

In June, I get a fun cube.

In June, I run on a big dune!

1. I cut a cute _____.

2. I hum a fab _____.

3. I ride a tan _____.

4. I get a fun _____.

5. I run on a big _____.

Long *Uu*

Name: _____ Date: _____

Directions: Circle the word that names each picture.

1.

tube

cute

cube

2.

queen

seen

teen

3.

done

bone

come

4.

late

gate

tape

5.

mole

hole

pole

6.

seed

feed

need

7.

rule

mule

June

8.

time

fine

lime

9.

note

dome

home

10.

pave

fate

cave

11.

hide

pine

tide

12.

tune

Duke

dune

Directions: Name each picture. Circle the long vowel sound you hear in each word.

1.

a e i o u

2.

a e i o u

3.

a e i o u

4.

a e i o u

5.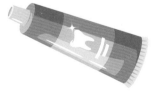

a e i o u

6.

a e i o u

7.

a e i o u

8.

a e i o u

9.

a e i o u

10.

a e i o u

Name: _____ Date: _____

Directions: Name each picture. Circle the letters you hear in each word. Blend the sounds, and write the word. Color the pictures. The first one has been done for you.

Say	Sounds		Write
	t (f) (e) u i (e) (t) f		**feet**
	k h a i t k e		
	c s o a k l e		
	m n e o t h e		
	l f o a t k e		
	v r u o p b e		
	k m e a o e l t		
	k c u i t d e		

Review: Long Vowels

Directions: Name each picture. Unscramble each word. Draw a line from each word to the matching picture.

1. n e c a _____

2. e k a r _____

3. e b e t _____

4. v e i h _____

5. i f v e _____

6. d e m o _____

7. u J e n _____

8. e u t n _____

Review: Long Vowels

WEEK 34
DAY
5

Name: _____   Date: _____

Directions: Put two game markers on **Start**. Take turns rolling a number cube with a partner. Move your game marker the number you roll. Say the word you land on. Use it in a sentence. The first player to land on **End** wins.

Review: Long Vowels

Start		teen	cube	**Lose a turn.**
tube		**Go back 2 spaces.**		bite
feed				take
ripe		tune		seed
cone		weed		**Go back to start.**
mole		pipe		
Go back to start.		rope		lime
game		**Go back 2 spaces.**		**Go back 3 spaces.**
rule	feel	**Lose a turn.**		**End**

© Shell Education

Overview

Cumulative Review: Consonants, Short Vowels, and CVC Words

In this unit, students will review the phonics skills they have learned so far. By learning the relationship between letters and the sounds they make, emerging readers can begin to decode words and identify patterns. Celebrate student successes, and encourage students to read as much as they can, both independently and with help.

Directions: Read the sentence. Draw a picture to go with the sentence.

The dog sat on a mat.

Name: _____ Date: _____

Directions: Name each picture. Write the letter you hear at the beginning of each word.

1. 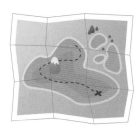 ___ ___

2.  ___ ___

3. 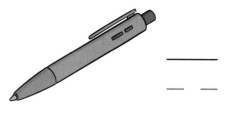 ___ ___

4.  ___ ___

5. 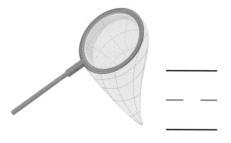 ___ ___

6.  ___ ___

7.  ___ ___

8.  ___ ___

9. 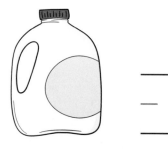 ___ ___

10.  ___ ___

Name: _____ Date: _____

Directions: Name each picture. Write the letter you hear at the end of each word.

1.  ___ ___ ___

4.  ___ ___ ___

2.  ___ ___ ___

5. ___ ___ ___

3.  ___ ___ ___

6.  ___ ___ ___

Directions: Name each picture. Write the short vowel you hear in each word.

7. ___ ___ ___

10.  ___ ___ ___

8. ___ ___ ___

11.  ___ ___ ___

9.  ___ ___ ___

12.  ___ ___ ___

Name: _____ Date: _____

Directions: Touch each dot, and say the sound. Write the word. Read the word. Circle whether each word is **real** or **nonsense**.

1.

f	i	x

● ● ●

_____

‒ ‒ ‒ ‒ ‒ ‒

_____

real

nonsense

2.

j	a	b

● ● ●

_____

‒ ‒ ‒ ‒ ‒ ‒

_____

real

nonsense

3.

v	o	k

● ● ●

_____

‒ ‒ ‒ ‒ ‒ ‒

_____

real

nonsense

4.

b	e	t

● ● ●

_____

‒ ‒ ‒ ‒ ‒ ‒

_____

real

nonsense

5.

qu	i	t

● ● ●

_____

‒ ‒ ‒ ‒ ‒ ‒

_____

real

nonsense

6.

z	u	m

● ● ●

_____

‒ ‒ ‒ ‒ ‒ ‒

_____

real

nonsense

Name: _____ Date: _____

Directions: Use the letters in each row to make short-vowel words. Write four words for each set of letters. Each word needs one vowel.

a	b	h	s	m	d

_____   _____

_____   _____

_____   _____

_____   _____

o	c	h	m	p	t	p

_____   _____

_____   _____

_____   _____

_____   _____

i	l	s	t	p	ck

_____   _____

_____   _____

_____   _____

_____   _____

Name: _____ Date: _____

Directions: Look at the pictures. Use the words to write sentences that match the pictures. Then, read the sentences aloud. **Note:** A sentence starts with a capital letter. A name starts with a capital letter.

Max

1.

| is | cub. | Max | a |

2.

| den. | Max | a | lives | in |

3.

| with | naps | Max | Mom. |

4.

| Max | mud. | in | plays |

5.

| a | fun | is | Max | cub! |

Directions: Get two colors of game markers. Take turns with a partner. Read a word on the board, and cover it with one of your markers. Play until one of you has four in a row.

Name: _____ Date: _____

Directions: Read each sentence. Circle the picture that matches the sentence.

1.

The kid can kick a bin.

2.

The wig is on a pig!

3.

Jim will sip with his lips.

4.

Rick hit it to win!

5.

The dog licks and sits.

Name: _____ Date: _____

Directions: Put two game markers on **Start**. Take turns rolling a number cube with a partner. Move your game marker the number of spaces you roll. Say the word on the space and a word that rhymes with it. You may use nonsense rhyming words. The first player to reach **End** is the winner.

Name: _____ Date: _____

Directions: Roll a number cube four times. Use the chart to write a silly sentence on another sheet of paper. Write five silly sentences. Read your silly sentences to a friend.

	Roll 1	Roll 2	Roll 3	Roll 4
 ⚀	The big	cub	sat	in a pit.
 ⚁	A wet	rat	hugs	on a sub.
 ⚂	The fun	dog	dips	in the mud.
 ⚃	A mad	hen	got	on the bus.
 ⚄	The red	pig	pecks	in a van.
 ⚅	A hot	fox	raps	on a bun.

Directions: Write your own story. Write two or three sentences. You can use the words in the box if you want. Draw a picture to go with your story.

bad	cat	fun	have	ride
big	cute	get	meet	run
can	dog	go	pal	time

_____

- -

_____

- -

_____

- -

_____

Standards Correlations

Shell Education is committed to producing educational materials that are research and standards based. To support this effort, this resource is correlated to the academic standards of all 50 states, the District of Columbia, the Department of Defense Dependent Schools, and the Canadian provinces. A correlation is also provided for key professional educational organizations.

To print a customized correlation report for your state, visit our website at **www.tcmpub.com/administrators/correlations** and follow the online directions. If you require assistance in printing correlation reports, please contact the Customer Service Department at 1-800-858-7339.

Standards Overview

The Every Student Succeeds Act (ESSA) mandates that all states adopt challenging academic standards that help students meet the goal of college and career readiness. While many states already adopted academic standards prior to ESSA, the act continues to hold states accountable for detailed and comprehensive standards. Standards are designed to focus instruction and guide adoption of curricula. They define the knowledge, skills, and content students should acquire at each level. Standards are also used to develop standardized tests to evaluate students' academic progress. State standards are used in the development of our resources, so educators can be assured they meet state academic requirements.

College and Career Readiness

Today's college and career readiness (CCR) standards offer guidelines for preparing K–12 students with the knowledge and skills that are necessary to succeed in postsecondary job training and education. CCR standards include the Common Core State Standards as well as other state-adopted standards such as the Texas Essential Knowledge and Skills. The standards found on page 201 describe the content presented throughout the lessons.

TESOL and WIDA Standards

English language development standards are integrated within each lesson to enable English learners to work toward proficiency in English while learning content—developing the skills and confidence in listening, speaking, reading, and writing. The standards found in the digital resources describe the language objectives presented throughout the lessons.

Standards Correlations *(cont.)*

180 Days™: Phonics for Kindergarten offers a full page of daily phonics practice activities for each day of the school year.

Every week provides practice activities tied to a variety of language arts standards, offering students the opportunity for regular practice in decoding, word recognition, phonics, reading, and writing.

Reading Foundation Skills
Recognize that spoken words are represented in written language by specific sequences of letters.
Understand that words are separated by spaces in print.
Recognize and name all upper- and lowercase letters of the alphabet.
Phonological Awareness
Demonstrate understanding of spoken words, syllables, and sounds (phonemes).
Recognize and produce rhyming words.
Count, pronounce, blend, and segment words into syllables in spoken words.
Blend and segment onsets and rimes of single-syllable spoken words.
Isolate and pronounce the initial, medial vowel, and final sounds (phonemes) in three-phoneme (consonant-vowel-consonant, or CVC) words.
Add or substitute individual sounds (phonemes) in simple, one-syllable words to make new words.
Phonics and Word Recognition
Know and apply grade-level phonics and word analysis skills in decoding words.
Demonstrate basic knowledge of one-to-one letter-sound correspondences by producing the primary sound or many of the most frequent sounds for each consonant.
Associate the long and short sounds with the common spellings (graphemes) for the five major vowels.
Distinguish between similarly spelled words by identifying the sounds of the letters that differ.
Reading Literature
With prompting and support, ask and answer questions about key details in text.
Ask and answer questions about unknown words in a text.

References Cited

Beck, Isabel L. and Mark E. Beck. 2013. *Making Sense of Phonics: The Hows and Whys, Second Edition*. New York: Guilford.

Marzano, Robert. 2010. "When Practice Makes Perfect Sense." *Educational Leadership* 68 (3): 81–83.

National Reading Panel. 2000. *Report of the National Reading Panel: Teaching Children to Read*. Report of the Subgroups. Washington, DC: U.S. Department of Health and Human Services, National Institutes of Health.

Answer Key

There are many open-ended prompts in this book. For those activities, answers will vary, and example answers are provided when possible.

Unit 1

Week 1
Day 1 (page 12)
Check that students have circled the first letter of each word.

Day 2 (page 13)
Check that students have circled the first letter of each word.

Day 3 (page 14)

Day 4 (page 15)

Check that students have written their names with a capital letter. Check that students have circled the first and last letters of their names.

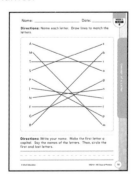

Day 5 (page 16)
1. c
2. l
3. h
4. r
5. d
6. t

Week 2
Day 1 (page 17)
Check that students have circled the first letter of each word and underlined each word.

Check that students have written their names and that the first and last letters are circled.

Day 2 (page 18)

Try This: *A* and *I*

Day 3 (page 19)
1. m
2. S
3. f
4. p
5. n
6. m
7. p
8. g

Day 4 (page 20)
1. (n)a(p)
2. (m)a(t)
3. (j)a(m)
4. (t)a(g)

First Letters	Last Letters
n	p
m	t
j	m
t	g

Day 5 (page 21)
1. doll
2. pencil
3. hat
4. cow
5. I**X**can**X**learn.
6. The**X**dog**X**jumps.
7. The**X**cat**X**naps.

Week 3
Day 1 (page 22)
1. fig
2. cab
3. ham
4. bed
5. rat
6. fin

Day 2 (page 23)

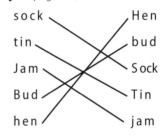

1. Pat likes jam.
2. He puts on a sock.
3. The hen eats.
4. His name is Bud.

Answer Key *(cont.)*

Day 3 (page 24)

The jar has a (lid)

(I) (met) a girl.

(Tom) likes the dog.

I can (run)

The cat is (big)

Did your hair get (wet)

Day 4 (page 25)

Check that the first and last word have been circled in each sentence.

1. map
2. red
3. cat
4. run
5. pup

Day 5 (page 26)

Check that students have circled the exclamation point.

6 words

Week 4

Day 1 (page 27)

Listen for students identifying the initial sound in each word.

Students should circle the vowels *Aa, Ee, Ii, Oo,* and *Uu*.

Day 2 (page 28)

Day 3 (page 29)

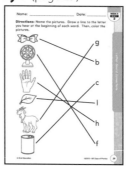

Day 4 (page 30)

Day 5 (page 31)

Unit 2

Week 5

Day 1 (page 33)

Students should circle the rabbit, stamp, hamster, tack, and van.

bag, nap

Day 2 (page 34)

Students should circle the apple, alligator, astronaut, and ax.

Day 3 (page 35)

1. | a | | |
2. | | a | |
3. | a | | |
4. | | a | |
5. | | a | |

Day 4 (page 36)

Answer Key (cont.)

Day 5 (page 37)

1. The(hat)is on the bed.
2. The(cat)(sat)
3. The(bat)(can)fly.
4. The(mat)is(black)

Week 6
Day 1 (page 38)

Day 2 (page 39)

1. m
2. t
3. m
4. t
5. t
6. m
7. m
8. t

Day 3 (page 40)

1. mat
2. ham
3. rat
4. cap

Day 4 (page 41)

1. tap
2. map
3. mat
4. Tam
5. the mat

Day 5 (page 42)

I am Tam.

My map is on a mat.

The mat is by the tub.

The map is wet.

I am mad.

Students should circle "The map is wet."

Week 7
Day 1 (page 43)

Starts with S	Starts with P
sat	pat
sap	Pam
Sam	

Day 2 (page 44)

S: seal, strawberry, soup

P: pickle, picture, pineapple

S: dress

P: sleep

Day 3 (page 45)

1. cap
2. Sal
3. tap
4. pal

Day 4 (page 46)

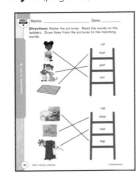

Day 5 (page 47)

Pat has a **cat**.

The cat has a red **mat**.

The cat takes a **nap** on the mat.

Did **Pat** nap with the cat?

No, he **sat**!

Week 8
Day 1 (page 48)

Day 2 (page 49)

1. monkey
2. peacock
3. spoon
4. table
5. six

Day 3 (page 50)

1. | m | a | t |
2. | m | a | p |
3. | t | a | p |
4. | s | a | t |
5. | s | a | p |

Day 4 (page 51)

Top: tap, map, sap

Bottom: pat, sat, mat

Answer Key *(cont.)*

Day 5 (page 52)

1. no
2. yes
3. no
4. yes

Unit 3

Week 9

Day 1 (page 54)

1. nip
2. sip
3. bit
4. sit
5. pit
6. Tim

Day 2 (page 55)

Day 3 (page 56)

1. Tim
2. sit
3. pit
4. tip

Day 4 (page 57)

Left: bit, sit, pit

Right: rip, sip, tip

Tim jumps over the pit.

Day 5 (page 58)

Pat can sit by the water.

She can sit by Tim on the mat.

Pat and Tim look at the map.

They see a pit on the map.

Short *a*	Short *i*
Pat	sit
can	Tim
mat	pit
map	
at	

Week 10

Day 1 (page 59)

1. f
2. f
3. n
4. f
5. n
6. f
7. n
8. n

Day 2 (page 60)

1. n
2. n
3. f
4. f
5. n
6. f
7. n
8. f

Day 3 (page 61)

1. | b | i | n |

2. | f | i | n |

3. | p | i | n |

4. | t | i | n |

5. | i | n |

Day 4 (page 62)

1. nap
2. fan
3. tip
4. man
5. mat
6. pan

Day 5 (page 63)

1. The bat can sit.
2. The pin is in a tin.
3. San has a tan fan.
4. Tan has the pit.

Week 11

Day 1 (page 64)

g: grass, grapes

b: baby, ball

n: nose, nuts

f: flower, frog

p: pig, popcorn

Answer Key *(cont.)*

Day 2 (page 65)

1. b
2. g
3. b
4. g
5. g
6. b
7. g
8. b
9. b
10. g

Day 3 (page 66)

1. big
2. bag
3. bin
4. gab
5. fig

Day 4 (page 67)

1. gap
2. pig
3. gab
4. fig
5. tag
6. bin
7. bag
8. big
9. tab

Day 5 (page 68)

Mag is a black **bat**.

She likes to gab with **San**.

She likes to **sit** with San.

She and San like **figs**.

Week 12

Day 1 (page 69)

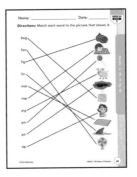

Day 2 (page 70)

1. n
2. p
3. g
4. f
5. b
6. m
7. b
8. g

Day 3 (page 71)

f	i	g

1.

b	i	g

2.

p	i	g

3.

p	i	t

4.

b	i	t

5.

Day 4 (page 72)

Left: wag, tag, bag

Right: bin, fin, pin

Day 5 (page 73)

Mag and San **sit** in the fig tree.

They see a **pig** by the tree.

Her name is **Nan**.

She will **nip** a fig.

Unit 4

Week 13

Day 1 (page 75)

Students should circle the log, mop, pot, and top.

The log has a pot on top.

Day 2 (page 76)

1. frog
2. bridge
3. flag
4. sock
5. mat
6. o
7. a
8. i
9. o
10. i
11. a

Day 3 (page 77)

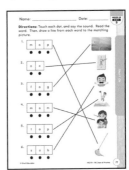

Answer Key *(cont.)*

Day 4 (page 78)

Left: pop, top, mop

Right: log, fog, bog

Day 5 (page 79)

Sam is a **dog**.

He walks by a **pit**.

Tom sits in the pit.

He **hops** to see Sam.

Week 14

Day 1 (page 80)

1. l
2. c
3. c
4. l
5. c
6. c
7. l
8. l
9. c
10. l

Day 2 (page 81)

Day 3 (page 82)

1. | c | o | b |
2. | l | a | p |
3. | p | a | l |
4. | l | a | b |
5. | c | o | t |

Day 4 (page 83)

1. top
2. lit
3. cob
4. cog
5. lip
6. cap

Day 5 (page 84)

Tom is a **pal** for Sam.

Tom says, "We can play **tag**."

Tom and Sam **jog** and jab.

Sam got **Tom**!

Week 15

Day 1 (page 85)

Hh: hop, hip, hanger, horse

Jj: jog, juice, juggle, jar, jellyfish

Day 2 (page 86)

1. ghost
2. frog
3. fan
4. cow
5. hammer
6. o
7. i
8. o
9. a

Day 3 (page 87)

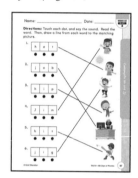

Day 4 (page 88)

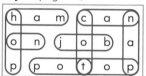

1. hop
2. cot
3. pot
4. job
5. can
6. on
7. nap
8. ham
9. top

Answer Key *(cont.)*

Day 5 (page 89)

Jan has a **job**.

She starts to **mop**.

But she has to **stop**.

It is too **hot**!

Week 16

Day 1 (page 90)

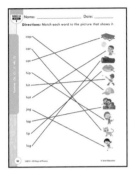

Day 2 (page 91)

1. hop
2. jog
3. cab
4. jam
5. log
6. lip
7. hit
8. lid

Day 3 (page 92)

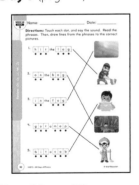

Day 4 (page 93)

Left: cot, tot, hot, pot

Right: sob, cob, job

Day 5 (page 94)

Ben is a **bug**.

He is not **big**.

He sits on a **log**.

He likes to **hop**.

Unit 5

Week 17

Day 1 (page 96)

Students should circle the bus, sun, nut, gum, and cup.

Gus, run, fun

Day 2 (page 97)

Day 3 (page 98)

1.	g	u	m
2.	t	u	b
3.	j	u	g
4.	b	u	n
5.	p	u	g
6.	t	u	g

Day 4 (page 99)

Left: nut, hut, cut

Right: hug, bug, pug, mug

Week 18

Day 1 (page 101)

1. r
2. k
3. r
4. r
5. k
6. r
7. k
8. k

Day 2 (page 102)

Students should circle the kite, kiss, kick, kitchen, and kitten.

Students should circle the duck, truck, and lock.

Day 3 (page 103)

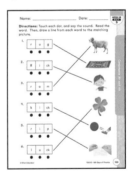

Answer Key (cont.)

Day 4 (page 104)

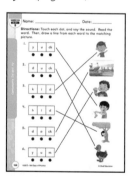

1. pick or pack
2. rat
3. pack or pick
4. rack
5. rip
6. run

Week 19

Day 1 (page 106)

1. d	6. d
2. d	7. y
3. y	8. y
4. d	9. d
5. y	10. y

Day 2 (page 107)

1. y	6. d
2. d	7. d
3. d	8. m
4. y	9. g
5. y	10. d

Day 3 (page 108)

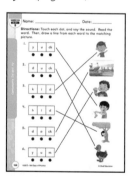

Day 4 (page 109)

Left: yuck, muck, duck

Right: pad, mad, sad, dad

Day 5 (page 110)

1. pug
2. duck
3. muck
4. bug
5. Yuck

Week 20

Day 1 (page 111)

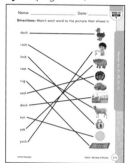

Day 2 (page 112)

1. cup
2. gum
3. rug
4. dog
5. rip
6. lock
7. ram
8. mug
9. back

Day 3 (page 113)

c	car
	cut
r	rock
	rug
d	duck
	dog
y	yam
	yum

Day 4 (page 114)

1. rack
2. arm
3. yip
4. kick
5. nut
6. kid
7. puck
8. sub
9. dot

Unit 6

Week 21

Day 1 (page 117)

Students should circle the sled, egg, ten, elephant, and tent.

Day 2 (page 118)

1. u	7. e
2. e	8. a
3. e	9. t
4. i	10. g
5. e	11. ck
6. o	12. n

Day 3 (page 119)

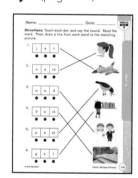

Day 4 (page 120)

Left: hen, men, Ken, pen

Right: wed, Ted, bed, red

Answer Key *(cont.)*

Day 5 (page 121)

Meg **met** her friend, Ren.

Meg **led** Ren to the rock.

Ren had a **sack**.

They **sat** on the rock.

Week 22

Day 1 (page 122)

1. qu
2. w
3. w
4. qu
5. w

6. w
7. qu
8. w
9. qu
10. w

Day 2 (page 123)

Day 3 (page 124)

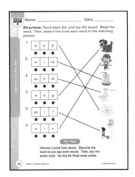

Day 4 (page 125)

1. win
2. wick
3. quit

4. quack
5. wig
6. web

Day 5 (page 126)

Dear **Meg**,

I am by a big **rock**.

I saw a **duck**.

I **fed** the duck.

It said, "**Quack**!"

Love, Ren

Week 23

Day 1 (page 127)

Vv: vet, vacuum, vest

Zz: zipper, zoo, zebra, zero

Xx: fox, box, six, mix

Day 2 (page 128)

1. zebra
2. fish
3. sun
4. vase

5. quack
6. net
7. zip
8. box

Day 3 (page 129)

1.	t	u	x
2.	z	i	p
3.	v	e	t
4.	f	i	x
5.	b	o	x

Day 4 (page 130)

Left: jet, wet, net, vet

Right: fix, mix

Day 5 (page 131)

1. fox
2. tux
3. mix
4. vet

Week 24

Day 1 (page 132)

Day 2 (page 133)

1. zip
2. vet
3. six
4. quack
5. wig
6. fix
7. tux
8. box

Day 3 (page 134)

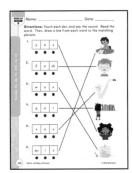

Day 4 (page 135)

1. yes
2. zip
3. net
4. mix
5. web
6. vet
7. fox
8. pen
9. wax

Answer Key (cont.)

Day 5 (page 136)
1. Max got a pet!
2. Her name is Wen.
3. Wen is quick!
4. Max can mix treats for Wen!

Unit 7

Week 25

Day 1 (page 138)

1.	yak	5.	mad
2.	wag	6.	bat
3.	sad	7.	map
4.	ran; cab	8.	pack

Day 2 (page 139)

1.	an	7.	ack
2.	ap	8.	ag
3.	am	9.	ad
4.	at	10.	am
5.	an	11.	ap
6.	ab	12.	ack

Day 3 (page 140)
1. yam/ham
2. nap/map
3. mat/hat
4. quack/sack
5. gab/cab

Day 4 (page 141)
Possible words include: pack, bat, tap, tack, back, bat, tab, sack, sat, sap, mat, map, bag, tag, cat, sag, cab, and cap.

Day 5 (page 142)
1. big ram
2. mad cat
3. bad van
4. sad rat
5. tan hat

Week 26

Day 1 (page 143)

1.	bit	5.	dig
2.	sick	6.	lid
3.	win	7.	kick
4.	wick	8.	pin

Day 2 (page 144)

1.	ig	7.	id
2.	in	8.	it
3.	it	9.	ip
4.	ip	10.	id
5.	ick	11.	in
6.	ix	12.	ix

Day 3 (page 145)
1. pick/sick
2. dig/wig
3. sip/hip
4. Kim/rim
5. win/pin

Day 4 (page 146)
Possible words include: sick, pick, sip, pit, tip, sit, pig, tick, kit, kick, bit, and big.

Day 5 (page 147)
1. Liz can sit.
2. Ben can hit.
3. Gus can sip.
4. Mel can lick.
5. Deb can kick.

Week 27

Day 1 (page 148)

1.	log	5.	sock
2.	dock	6.	cot
3.	top	7.	mom
4.	jog	8.	rock

Day 2 (page 149)

1.	ock	7.	ot
2.	om	8.	ot
3.	op	9.	og
4.	ob	10.	ock
5.	ox	11.	ob
6.	op	12.	ox

Day 3 (page 150)
1. sock/dock
2. mop/pop
3. pot/hot
4. dog/log
5. job/cob

Day 4 (page 151)
Possible words include: tock, rock, rot, mop, pot, top, hop, got, hot, hog, log, and lock.

Day 5 (page 152)
1. big sock
2. tan log
3. top cot
4. fun mom
5. wet jog

Week 28

Day 1 (page 153)

1.	gum	5.	sub
2.	sun	6.	cut
3.	bus	7.	duck
4.	pup; tub	8.	cup

Day 2 (page 154)

1.	ug	7.	ug
2.	uck	8.	up
3.	ub	9.	un
4.	un	10.	us
5.	ut	11.	ut
6.	uck	12.	ug

Answer Key *(cont.)*

Day 3 (page 155)

1. cup/pup
2. luck/yuck
3. sub/cub
4. pug/bug
5. sun/bun

Day 4 (page 156)

Possible words include: yuck, yum, muck, gum, mug, tug, gut, tub, hut, but, hug, buck, bug, cut, and cub.

Day 5 (page 157)

1. Dan can run.
2. Tom can cut.
3. Kim can hug.
4. Gus can sit in the tub.
5. Pam can have fun.

Week 29

Day 1 (page 158)

1. bed
2. fed
3. wet
4. leg
5. hen
6. web
7. net
8. ten

Day 2 (page 159)

1. ed
2. eg
3. eb
4. eck
5. en
6. eg
7. et
8. en
9. eck
10. ed
11. en
12. et

Day 3 (page 160)

1. bed/red
2. ten/men
3. neck/peck
4. wet/net
5. Meg/leg

Day 4 (page 161)

Possible words include: bed, deck, vet, peck, ten, net, neck, pet, pen, wet, web, and bet.

Day 5 (page 162)

1. red pen
2. hot mug
3. big deck
4. tan bed
5. red jet

Week 30

Day 1 (page 163)

buck	fit	Deb	set	fed	Peg
pen	sack	bid	mad	dab	did
fib	tack	pick	sob	tot	mix
mop	fix	pad	tick	bed	tax

Day 2 (page 164)

1. u
2. a
3. i
4. u
5. e
6. u
7. i
8. o

Day 3 (page 165)

1. fan
2. rip
3. quick
4. mud
5. dig
6. box
7. leg
8. yam

Day 4 (page 166)

1. dot
2. hat
3. kick
4. gum
5. hot
6. wig
7. hen
8. yum
9. ten
10. ram

Day 5 (page 167)

1. What is in the box?
2. Ron can tip it.
3. Ron's mom can cut the box.
4. Ron can hug it!

Unit 8

Week 31

Day 1 (page 169)

Day 2 (page 170)

i	i	a
a	i	a
i	a	a

short	long
long	short

Day 3 (page 171)

1. | r | a | k | e | rake
2. | l | a | k | e | lake
3. | t | a | p | e | tape
4. | f | i | v | e | five
5. | r | i | d | e | ride
6. | p | i | p | e | pipe

Answer Key *(cont.)*

Day 4 (page 172)

1. hive
2. cave
3. pipe
4. hide
5. cane
6. bite
7. maze

Day 5 (page 173)

These words should be circled:
kite, bite, bus, us, lime, time.

Week 32

Day 1 (page 174)

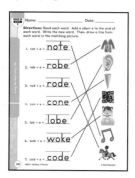

Day 2 (page 175)

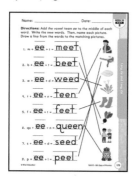

Day 3 (page 176)

1.	h	o	l	e	hole
2.	b	o	n	e	bone
3.	h	o	m	e	home
4.	l	ee	k		leek
5.	w	ee	d		weed
6.	qu	ee	n		queen

Day 4 (page 177)

note

cone

code

rope

Left: beet, feet

Right: seed, weed

Day 5 (page 178)

Pete has a big **home**.

We can take a **peek**!

It is not a **hole**.

It is **deep**.

Pete **made** it.

It is a dam!

Week 33

Day 1 (page 179)

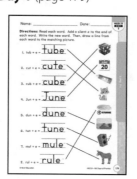

Day 2 (page 180)

1.	short	5.	long
2.	long	6.	long
3.	long	7.	short
4.	short	8.	long

Day 3 (page 181)

1.	mule	4.	cube
2.	June	5.	tube
3.	tune	6.	cute

Day 5 (page 183)

1. cake
2. tune
3. mule
4. cube
5. dune

Week 34

Day 1 (page 184)

1.	cube	7.	mule
2.	teen	8.	lime
3.	bone	9.	home
4.	gate	10.	cave
5.	mole	11.	hide
6.	seed	12.	tune

Day 2 (page 185)

1.	a	6.	i
2.	o	7.	e
3.	u	8.	o
4.	i	9.	a
5.	u	10.	e

Answer Key *(cont.)*

Day 3 (page 186)

1. feet
2. hike
3. cake
4. note
5. lake
6. robe
7. meet
8. cute

Day 4 (page 187)

Unit 9

Week 35

Day 1 (page 190)

1. m
2. c
3. p
4. f
5. n
6. l
7. v
8. y
9. j
10. b

Day 2 (page 191)

1. g
2. d
3. n
4. s
5. x
6. b
7. o
8. u
9. i
10. u
11. e
12. a

Day 3 (page 192)

1. fix; real
2. jab; real
3. vok; nonsense
4. bet; real
5. quit; real
6. zum; nonsense

Day 4 (page 193)

Possible words include:

bad, had, sad, mad, dad, bam, dam

cop, hop, mop, pop, top, hot, cot

lick, sick, tick, pick, tip, pit, sit, lip

Day 5 (page 194)

1. Max is a cub.
2. Max lives in a den.
3. Max naps with Mom.
4. Max plays in mud.
5. Max is a fun cub!

Week 36

Day 2 (page 196)

Digital Resources

Accessing the Digital Resources

The digital resources can be downloaded by following these steps:

1. Go to **www.tcmpub.com/digital**

2. Use the 13-digit ISBN number to redeem the digital resources.

3. Respond to the question using the book.

4. Follow the prompts on the Content Cloud website to sign in or create a new account.

5. The content redeemed will now be on your My Content screen. Click on the product to look through the digital resources. All resources are available for download. Select files can be previewed, opened, and shared.

For questions and assistance with your ISBN redemption, please contact Teacher Created Materials.

> **email:** customerservice@tcmpub.com

> **phone:** 800-858-7339

Contents of the Digital Resources

- Standards Correlations

- Class and Individual Analysis Sheets

- Hands-On Letter Practice

- Writing Practice